ULYSSES, THE WASTE LAND, and MODERNISM

Kennikat Press
National University Publications
Literary Criticism Series

General Editor
John E. Becker
Fairleigh Dickinson University

STANLEY SULTAN

ULYSSES, THE WASTE LAND, and MODERNISM

A Jubilee Study

National University Publications
KENNIKAT PRESS   //   1977
Port Washington, N. Y.   //   London

Manufactured in the United States of America

Published by
Kennikat Press Corp.
Port Washington, N. Y. / London

Library of Congress Cataloging in Publication Data

Sultan, Stanley.
  Ulysses, The waste land, and modernism.

  (National university publications)
  Includes bibliographical references and index.
  1. Joyce, James, 1882-1941. Ulysses. 2. Eliot,
Thomas Stearns, 1888-1965. The waste land. 3.
Modernism (Literature) I. Title.
PR6019.09U735   823'.9'12   76-22553
ISBN 0-8046-9144-4

This book is dedicated to my mother
BESS LEINWAND SULTAN

ACKNOWLEDGMENTS

This book originated in a set of lectures on *Ulysses* and *The Waste Land* that I delivered at the State University of New York at Binghamton in 1972. In a sense its begetter was Professor Zack Bowen, who extended the invitation to lecture there, and I am happy for the opportunity to record my thanks to him.

Thanks are due as well, for help of various kinds, to James Franklin Beard, William H. Carter, Jr., Ella Conger, Linda Damslet, James P. Elliott, Mary Ann Heath, Serena Sue Hilsinger, Edmund Honig, Hugh Kenner, Dawn Kidd, A. Walton Litz, Arthur Pell, Theresa M. Reynolds, Betty Hillman Sultan, James L. Sultan and Lola L. Szladits.

CONTENTS

PREFACE

This book has three subjects. In order of increasing particularity they are: Modernism as an event and a condition of Western culture; the relationship between two famous modernist works; and the nature of one of those works. Catalogued, they seem more or less distinct from one another. But (to reverse the order) certain qualities of *The Waste Land* placed in a certain light reflect a rich set of similarities between it and *Ulysses*, and that set of similarities illuminates Modernism as a whole.

The path of this study will not, however, begin with a consideration of the poem and then move from most specific, to mediate, to most general of the three subjects, taking the reader on an expedition from base *Waste Land* to destination Modernism. Although the ground covered will be as described, that simple progress would, in my opinion, blaze a false trail.

My own thinking certainly did not proceed in that line. It began with a vague apprehension of similarity between the two works and moved in both directions: toward general implications of that similarity and (with the help of my previous work on *Ulysses*) toward what I believe to be greater understanding of the poem, especially of such cruxes of difficulty for critics and readers as its resolution, the status of the Notes, and the apparent incoherence caused by a great multiplicity of speakers. Then consideration of Modernism and of *The Waste Land* led me back to a greater awareness of the range and nature of the similarities between novel and poem. For me "the way up and the way down," though not the same, were part of the same process.

Of course, the form of an exposition cannot be justified on grounds of mental biography, and this study does not retrace the steps of the process. However, the relationship of my three subjects, clarified in the process of my thinking, is expressed in the form of this study. The context of each is the other two. The mutual illumination that links them moves both from and to the general and particular, and both out from and in to the middle. Finally, each is important in its own right; and if my limited observations about Modernism are only one blind man's account of the elephant, perhaps that grand subject has lifted me to a better view of the two lesser ones.

ULYSSES, THE WASTE LAND, and MODERNISM

1

OUR MODERN EXPERIMENT

*I hold this book to be the most important expression
which the present age has found.*
                     T. S. Eliot, "Ulysses, Order, and Myth"

The title *"Ulysses, The Waste Land,* and Modernism" is modeled on the
title of the benedictory essay written by the author of the second celebrated work it names about the first one soon after the publication of
both—an essay whose very existence makes it a document of cultural
significance; my subtitle employs the original Hebrew meaning of that
abused word *jubilee.* Although it derives from the (some say onomatopo-
etic) word for the sounding of horns, and the occasion was a joyous one,
the year following a week of weeks of years (on the Pentecostal model)
brought, according to *Leviticus* at least, a taking stock, a sorting out, and a
restoration of property to its original holders.

From the moment each appeared in 1922, *Ulysses* and *The Waste Land*
began to enjoy or suffer from one common distinction: an almost universal
characterization as the epitome in English of, respectively, the modernist
novel and the modernist poem. And because the familiar tends to seem
self-evident, for fifty years this singular characterization has persisted,
until today they are designated twin "myths" of Modernism.[1] This characterization has persisted although it ignores the general question of
whether or not a truly typical work can be found in any movement or
period, ignores the specific fact that one attribute of the movement that

3

began early in, and the period that occupied much of, this century is a great range of variety, and (outweighing both these sophisticated considerations) ignores the simple reality. It is simply true that if a case might be made respecting certain modernist works, perhaps even lesser works of these two writers (such as "The Dead" and "Gerontion"), neither *Ulysses* nor *The Waste Land* is really typical of modernist novels or poems. Therefore the distinction is strange; in addition, it is significantly revealing about Modernism, as I shall try to show.

The jubilee has come round. It is time (slightly past time) for a taking stock of our culture's response over half a century to these two works, a sorting out of elements common to both that would help to explain this response, and even a restoration of property.

Perhaps it is best to begin by acknowledging the possible objection that the use in my title—that all recent use—of the term Modernism begs two questions. One is whether or not the art of Eliot's "present age" can be characterized properly as that of a distinct movement and period in literary history having its own set of doctrines and practices, thereby warranting the status of *-ism*. The other is whether or not there is any justification for appropriating the body of the term, capitalizing it, and so to some extent compromising its former usefulness for simple temporal signification, all in order to create an awkward neologism.

Awkward it may be, but the term is not new. It actually was used pejoratively by Swift in a letter to Pope (23 July 1737) to designate the doctrines and practices of one side in the "Ancients and Moderns" dispute. During the decade when *Ulysses* and *The Waste Land* appeared, Laura Riding and Robert Graves, as well as John Crowe Ransom, used it in speaking of the art of that "present age"; in 1935 Janko Lavrin published a study of various twentieth-century European writers under the title *Aspects of Modernism*, and his Prefatory Note began by calling the term "hackneyed"; it was by no means so, but can be found occasionally in other criticism of the same and the next decade, to designate precisely the characteristic doctrines and practices of a movement and period to which *Ulysses* and *The Waste Land* belong. The currency of both the concept and that name has grown gradually since. Although none of the six glossaries of literary terms published during the last dozen years which I checked listed "Modernism," books and essays have begun appearing whose primary or exclusive purpose is to delineate a historical movement and period of history to which they give that name; and the Autumn 1971 issue of *New Literary History*, an intelligent periodical with full academic credentials, was devoted to

"Modernism and Postmodernism," and so not only declared as fact the finite and historical nature of the former, but called attention to the need of finding one day a name for the period we purportedly are now in.

Increasing currency does not, of course, denote universal acceptance. Resistance to innovation in literary history—to a new conception about art and culture that upsets the received dogma, and even to a seemingly new coinage—is to be expected; this resistance is unimportant by its nature, and transitory. But thoughtful critics too have rejected both the name *Modernism* and the very conception of a delineable period; and to ignore their judgment would be both discourteous and irresponsible. However, I shall defer discussing their objections until the concluding section of this study, when the substantive grounds of a positive argument will have been presented and at which point the subject will be most relevant.

If categorical rejection of Modernism is set aside temporarily, there remain disagreements with the delineation of a single most recent period in the past history of our culture. In "The Modern Apocalypse," Frank Kermode describes "two phases of modernism, our own and that of fifty years ago," a tradition-oriented strain and an antitraditional one, with the period of the first having ended.[2] Where Professor Kermode distinguishes two finite periods of Modernism, Harold Rosenberg sees none. For him there has been rather the defeat of history by modernity in a transcendence of periods during the past century. In *The Tradition of the New* (New York: McGraw-Hill, 1959), he writes of "an art whose history, regardless of the credos of its practitioners, has consisted of leaps from vanguard to vanguard . . ." (p. 11).

Literary movements can have unforeseen consequences. And literary periods—to the extent that those constructions of our historical imaginations exist and are not merely noumenal formulations—do not end and begin with the closing and opening of a curtain, as anyone who has tried to trace the "true beginning" of a period knows. Furthermore, they are myths, persuasive accounts of reality that are neither demonstrable fact nor demonstrable fiction, and valuable to us only if we are their masters, not their slaves.

Keeping these various notions in mind, I should classify Mr. Rosenberg's thesis alongside the conventional wisdom: as essentially avoiding the issue. Regarding Professor Kermode's opposite alternative to a single most recent period in the past history of our culture, it can be said with considerable justice that the vitalist spirit expressed in much of our culture today is a modernist romanticism in the normative senses of both terms (*romantic* and striving for *modernity*), whatever its historical relationship to Modernism, and at any rate *grew out of* the aspect of Modernism which Professor Kermode says is "our own" and calls "anti-traditional": that in fact Modernism had opposing tendencies,[3] reflected in the difference between Pound's earlier poetry and his later *Cantos*, or between Joyce's two novels and *Finnegans Wake*. The former tendency was Apollonian or controlled or intellectual or classical or formalist or animus or yang; the other was Dionysiac or unrestrained or sensual or romantic or aleatory or anima or yin. One is expressed in the title of a collection of Pound's essays, *Make It New*. "Remake what we have been given," this tendency seemed to assert, "conceive our art in a different and enlarged way, and so transcend fashions and work in terms of its essential nature, toward the limits if need be of that nature." The other tendency approaches a current view: "Let It (all) Hang (out)."

This discrimination of two opposed tendencies in Modernism is relevant here first because it suggests that *Ulysses* and *The Waste Land* are likely to embody the dominant "traditional" one primarily, if only because for half a century they have been regarded as epitomes of their "present age," of Modernism itself, and not as directly antecedent to our own Beckett and Burroughs, Orlovitz and Olson.[4] And it is relevant because of Ezra Pound. Pound's later work *is* directly antecedent to Orlovitz and Olson, for remarkably he seems to have influenced two successive and contrasting periods in English poetry.

The popular conception of Pound is of a poet unfortunately distracted (in both senses of the word) by economics, then led by that obsession with gold and usury to notorious politics. His political history makes the thought seem bizarre at first, but Pound's economics may well derive from an aesthetically based socialism in the tradition of the early William Morris and of Oscar Wilde. Apparently irrelevant ideas of his coalesce in the ethos of a culturally rich and socialist civilization: value is created by the work of human beings, and the work of the artist creates the greatest value, beauty; in the art of poetry, rhetoric corresponds to usury in society—it evades work and spuriously breeds a debased product—while the image (by the later *Cantos* the very words heard or read) is the honest coinage of reality.

For one zealous to have civilization fulfill itself in both beauty and justice, right action involves the militant refinement of taste as well as of statecraft; and during his earlier years the assayer's son who would develop an obsession with gold was both a remarkable appraiser of precious literary metal and a militant partisan of those who worked it. The historical context within which *Ulysses, The Waste Land* and Modernism are to be considered includes him as a central figure.

If the myth of a recently ended period in the history of our culture is indeed viable—and at the very least it would seem difficult for anyone who has lived in an industrialized Western country during the last dozen years to doubt that cultures can pass through distinct phases—then Modernism probably resulted (in literature in English, at least) from the advent of a movement, as new periods often do. They do so because, unlike a "school," or group of artists who evolve and follow a special fashion that does not violate the character of an existent period, a "movement," when the term is used in speaking of the arts, seems to be a profound dialectical antithesis to a period which develops during the period. If the movement prevails, it does so only in the sense that the new period that is created results from the dialectical confrontation of the movement with the old period, is a synthesis of former period and antithetical movement. For the artists of the movement were bred in and to some extent by the period: good art never matches its manifestos. A poet of my acquaintance whose work is now in fashion illustrates my point. When he began writing as an under-graduate more than a quarter of a century ago, he regarded his poetry as of its time—"modern." In certain respects, it was; yet to a greater and in-creasing extent it belonged to the inchoate antithetical movement within Modernism that drew upon such manifestations of the recessive tendency of Modernism as Pound's later poetry, and dialectically created our current period. As I understand the term, a movement is *a consensus of artists—and their allies—who work, some of them independently and even in isolation, some with and some without conscious intention, to effect a fundamental change in the established conception of their particular genre of art, and of reality insofar as that genre engages reality.*

To entitle an ambitious study of art and culture in the early part of this century *The Pound Era*, as Hugh Kenner has recently done, is not paro-chialism but justice, which is to say, good history. As time goes on, the young Ezra Pound is seen to be more and more influential as a compound of revolutionary leader and midwife of the modernist movement. For this role he may be indebted to a master who had recently proven that in the arts a human mover can make things happen. He was intimately associated with Yeats from the early years of the century, and in two decades Yeats, undeterred by the failure of predecessors, had created a self-conscious na-tional English literature in Ireland: reviewing books of Anglo-Irish writers; producing a constant stream of newspaper and magazine articles that exhorted Irish writers to use certain material and to work in certain ways, and Irish readers to buy, read and recommend certain writers; printing lists of best Irish books; persuading publishers to put out works on Ireland or by Irishmen; organizing literary societies and two theatrical groups, the second of which made history in its own right; starting special periodicals; prodding Irish intellectuals to do books of translation from the Irish and of Irish folklore, Irish history, Irish social studies; encouraging and attempting to promote the careers of Irish writers. Yeats began that activity at about the time Joyce began his schooling; yet, before his college years were over, Joyce could treat a fully Irish literature and drama in English, in a piece like "The Day of the Rabblement," as cultural fact. Yeats was not alone, of course; and it is a historical irony that, despite the advent of Synge and a number of lesser figures as a direct result of the movement, he was also its chief embellishment; but most people who have written on the subject agree that an Irish literature in English as self-conscious as American literature exists, and that it woud not have come about when it did— if at all—without his efforts.

Sometimes in concert with Yeats (when each was not busy working on the other to reform him in his own image), and with Eliot and others as well, but uniquely committed, Pound set himself to the same sort of work on behalf of the kind of literature (and music, painting, sculpture, art theory) he was determined to move forward. His field of English literary activity alone was a web of vocational and personal relationships: Yeats, Conrad and Stein; influential figures like H. L. Mencken, Amy Lowell, T. E. Hulme, Herbert Read, Wyndham Lewis and Roger Fry; such now-celebrated younger writers as Eliot, Woolf, Ford, Lawrence, Joyce, Forster, Hemingway, Frost, Cummings, Moore and Williams; and many lesser figures. That web, centered in Paris and London and reaching across the ocean, was itself the fabric of a modernist movement. He arranged for publication, sought out writers, wrote manifestos, organized splinter movements, raised money for writers, preached and exhorted.

A promotional reference to *The Waste Land* before its publication, in a letter to Felix E. Schelling, suggests Pound's awareness of what he was about: "Eliot's *Waste Land* is I think the justification of the 'movement,' of our modern experiment, since 1900."[5] Despite the facetiousness, this is no less true of his occasionally using "p. s. U. " (*post scriptum Ulixi*) in place of "A. D." and dating accordingly, as though with Joyce's completion of *Ulysses* "our modern experiment" had established a new, post-Christian, era.[6] The two testimonials also combine neatly to suggest his direct relevance to a discussion of *Ulysses, The Waste Land* and Modernism. This promoter of Modernism promoted and assisted no writer more than he did Joyce and Eliot.

To Harriet Monroe he wrote soon after he discovered Eliot in September 1914 that the young poet "has actually trained himself *and* modernized himself *on his own*"[7] ; and he cajoled and threatened her until she printed "Prufrock" in *Poetry* magazine. To Amy Lowell in the same year, when both were almost totally unknown, he wrote, "I think Lawrence and Joyce are the two strongest prose writers among les jeunes, and all the [older writers] are about played out."[8] (Yeats had shown him some of Joyce's early work toward the end of 1913 and he had promptly written to the stiff and introverted stranger offering his help.) To H. L. Mencken he wrote the following February, "The prose writer I am really interested in is James Joyce," and went on to describe Edgar Lee Masters (with strong reservations) and Eliot as "the most hopeful American poets."[9] He raised money for both writers, arranged publication for their work, and wrote a number of essays praising it. He helped Eliot compile his first volume, *Prufrock and Other Observations,* and then, when no publisher was found, borrowed the money to sponsor its publication (without the poet's knowledge).[10] And with *Ulysses* and *The Waste Land* his sponsorship of the writers reached its culmination. The exquisite literary sensor that had distinguished the genius of Yeats during his early manner, and the genius of Frost, Hemingway, Williams, Lawrence, Joyce, and Eliot, distinguished and celebrated those two works as masterpieces of what is now being called Modernism.

The historical ties of *Ulysses* with the modernist movement fashioned by Pound end here; those of *The Waste Land*, of course, do not. In 1925 Eliot added the dedication, his famous homage to Pound. The fact of Pound's influence on the final form of the poem has long been known from the letters he exchanged with Eliot. And that that influence was as extensive as many said has been confirmed by the recently published drafts. Although Eliot made his own decisions, he seems usually (until a crucial development, as I shall endeavor to show) to have followed Pound's recommendations. These produced not just dramatic cuts and verbal refinements but the constant breaking of what was predominantly regular verse—the getting, as Pound declared his aim for English poetry in general to be, of Milton off Eliot's back.[11] And as a consequence, among Eliot's poems *The Waste Land* is most like Pound's own mature poetry. Yeats had set Synge to work as a writer in order to effect his larger purpose; Pound did Yeats one better with *The Waste Land*.

Much of this has been simplified literary history, but it is the necessary starting point. At the time he was writing essays about *Ulysses* and its literary antecedents through James and Flaubert to Homer, Pound was recasting his early *Cantos* to focus on Homer and Odysseus.[12] Likewise, one can cite specific artistic strategies inspired by *Ulysses* in the work of, for example, Faulkner and Dos Passos, and by *The Waste Land* in that of Crane and MacLeish; furthermore, both of them served as marks for other writers to aim at, as high and inspiring accomplishments of the powerful new movement in art. But in fact neither one was directly influential on very much other modernist literature, just as neither can be said to be typical— again, contrary to the familiar inherited presumption. Why then do they occupy their unique place as the modernist novel and poem in English that first come to mind, the works that are continually cited as examples by critics, in the way *Oedipus* and Dante, *Hamlet* and *The Rape of the Lock*, *Faust* and *Anna Karenina* are cited? Certainly it is not a matter of excellence; few would place precisely those two modernist works alone together on a pinnacle above all others. Yet no educated person of my generation, at least, can fail to have a culturally conditioned response to the naming of either one, or would be surprised to find a play produced at the end of their jubilee year presenting them as primary formative influences on a black American writer-intellectual (and the Leopold Bloom of his imagination as a character).[13] What is their kinship with each other and with their era?

2

THE SPELL OF *ULYSSES*

*It is a book to which we are all indebted, and from
which none of us can escape.*

Literary influence can work in strange ways. Herbert Howarth has pointed
out that the English text of the famous lecture introducing *Ulysses* given
by the prestigious French critic and editor Valéry Larbaud appeared in the
inaugural issue of Eliot's magazine *Criterion* (October 1922) in company
with the editor's new poem *The Waste Land*, that the issue also contained
an essay by Yeats's friend T. Sturge Moore complaining of the neglect of
the (Celtic) legend of Tristram and Iseult, and that the next spring Joyce
drafted the Tristram fragment of his new work which was to be *Finnegans
Wake*.[14] Eliot himself, however, seems to have had no discernible influence
on Joyce, unless the poet's coincidental brief use of Wagner's version of
the legend in *The Waste Land* reinforced Moore. Always a shrewd publicist,
Joyce welcomed Eliot's arranging to print a translation of Larbaud; and he
recruited Eliot to write about his use of myth, as he recruited Larbaud to
write about his formal devices and Pound to write about the range of his
vision. He apparently did not like Eliot's work until *The Waste Land* and is
reported to have said after reading it, "I had never realized Eliot was a
poet"[15] ; he undoubtedly "realized" a great deal more about the poem,
which I shall get to.

The reverse was not the case. From the time he wrote whetting readers'
appetites for *Ulysses* in the *Egoist* of June-July 1918 and praising "the

later work of Mr. James Joyce" in the *Atheneum* of July 4, 1919, through his calling Joyce the greatest master of the English language since Milton about fifteen years later, to the designation of *Ulysses* as "the most considerable work of imagination in English in our time" in his eloquent response to the mean and stupid obituary of Joyce printed by the London *Times* ("A Message to the Fish"), which they did not publish, Eliot was an outspoken admirer of Joyce's art, and of that work especially.[16] But as the passage from "Ulysses, Order, and Myth" quoted at the head of this section suggests, an admired colleague can become an influential master, and therefore a threat.

Joyce made certain that the chapters of *Ulysses* were read in typescript by his patron Harriet Weaver, his good friend in Trieste Frank Budgen, his two eager publicists Valéry Larbaud and Ezra Pound— and finally by his newer admirer, Pound's friend T. S. Eliot.[17] Virginia Woolf later recollected what Eliot had said about *Ulysses*, apparently just after he had finished the Notes of *The Waste Land:* "How could anyone write again after achieving the immense prodigy of the last chapter? [Eliot] was, for the first time in my knowledge, rapt, enthusiastic."[18] Echoing "from which none of us can escape," he wrote to Joyce of *Ulysses* on May 21, 1921, during the time he was working on his poem, "I wish, for my own sake, that I had not read it."[19] And less than two weeks earlier he had written to his (and Joyce's) patron, "the man from New York," John Quinn, "the latter part of *Ulysses*, which I have been reading in manuscript, is truly magnificent," and gone on in the same letter to speak of "a long poem [apparently his customary way of referring to *The Waste Land* before its completion] in mind and partly on paper which I am wishful to finish." As we know, he wrote most of it half a year later, "when I was at Lausanne for treatment."[20]

No doubt the burden of all this is apparent; furthermore, some of the dozens of allusions in *Finnegans Wake* to *The Waste Land*, Eliot and Eliot's other poetry represent Eliot as having derived *The Waste Land* from *Ulysses*. Joyce makes him a Shaun type and rival. He seems to have regarded the two of them as competitors with *Ulysses* and *The Waste Land*, and Eliot as guilty both of filching some of his thunder—appropriating fame that was rightly his—and plagiarizing from his novel, with inferior results.[21] Such a representation is not only ungenerous but also unfair, in my opinion, especially since no one appropriated more or was lionized more than the author of *Ulysses*. Yet, on the other side of the scale, in *Finnegans Wake* Joyce treats everyone, above all himself, with hyperbolic disrespect; and his feelings probably are equally well represented by a genial parody of *The Waste Land* that he sent to Harriet Shaw Weaver.[22]

Eliot had written of the significance of "the way in which a poet borrows" to argue the inferiority of Philip Massinger in an essay published while he was working on *The Waste Land* and Joyce was working on *Ulysses*. The passage is a familiar one, and declares that the charge of plagiarism in itself would not have perturbed him: "Immature poets imitate; mature poets steal; bad poets deface what they take, and good poets make it into something better, or at least something different."[23] However, one who simply steals is not threatened by that which he plunders; and there are certain similarities between the two works that document Eliot's sheer inability to escape from the spell of *Ulysses*. There are also significant differences, however. Finally, there are similarities which go deeper than the conscious or unconscious impress of one artist's work on that of another, and which may be the manifestation of a phase of culture. In a letter written to Eliot when they both were older, Joyce spoke of "what we are all trying in our different ways to do."[24] His reference to an "all" provides an interesting reflection of what has already been said about Modernism; the predicate of his clause projects us into further considerations: (1) How truly different were the "ways" of the writer and the recipient of that letter in their respective works of fifty years ago? and (2) What light do those two works cast on "what" it was the modernists were all "trying to do"?

3

A QUESTION OF INFLUENCE

> *Of course, the influence which Mr. Joyce's book may*
> *have is from my point of view an irrelevance.*

Anyone aware that the author of *The Waste Land* had written an essay commending the author of *Ulysses* for his use of myth should be alert for signs of influence; and while, understandably, students of Joyce have shown little concern,[25] a good deal of attention has been paid by students of Eliot and of modernist literature generally. Most have concentrated on the use of myth in the two works and mentioned incidental specific details of *The Waste Land* that seem to be borrowings.[26] The major source adduced for these borrowings is the third chapter of the novel—which in fact, as one of the chapters published in the *Egoist*, would have been read with special care by that journal's literary editor, T. S. Eliot.

In that chapter, as I have tried to show elsewhere,[27] Stephen wrestles with his thought through its many changes (an analogy with Menelaus, who in the *Odyssey* tells Telemachus how he wrestled with Proteus in order to learn how to escape from an island on which he had become becalmed); he is searching for escape from his physical and emotional situation. Stephen's self-confrontation grows out of and circles about the question whether all of his dead mother is buried or she has a resurrected soul—and he himself has a soul—until it becomes a confrontation with his past life and the impasse to which that life has brought him.

At least two specific elements of the chapter (both of them developments out of the preceding chapter) are similar to elements of *The Waste Land*: that of the drowned man and drowned dog ("Death by Water"); and that of the gypsy's dog's digging, which Stephen likens to the "fox burying his grandmother" of the riddle he had told his pupils in a compulsive way. The fox-dog of Stephen's thoughts is not burying but attempting to dig up, to see if indeed his (grand)mother has gone, as the riddle says, "to heaven." Even including its spiritual concern, the element seems a direct influence on the end of "The Burial of the Dead":

> That corpse you planted in your garden,
> Has it begun to sprout? Will it bloom this year?
> Or has the sudden frost disturbed its bed?
> Oh keep the Dog far hence, that's friend to men,
> Or with his nails he'll dig it up again!

Some twenty years ago Giorgio Melchiori published in Europe the first study devoted to establishing and exploring the influence of *Ulysses* on *The Waste Land*.[28] Professor Melchiori's essay "centres ... mainly on the third" chapter, and in it he traces the dog imagery in Eliot's work and concludes that for Eliot a dog is "the busy enquirer who founds his search on areligious, or rather on purely animal bases"[29]; interestingly, he fails to note what first struck me about Eliot's apparent appropriation from Joyce —that "Dog" is capitalized and therefore presented in an orthographic pun as the opposite of "God," a significantly narrowed derivation from Joyce's portrayal of an "Adonai" who, in Stephen's fantasy of a black mass in nighttown, responds to "the voice of all the damned" according to their conception of Him: "Dooooooooooog!" before responding to "the voice of all the blessed" with the "g" before and the "d" after the eleven "o"s.

The essay mentions additional similarities of motif or image, then turns to verbal "borrowings," which the author believes were consciously "stolen," to use Eliot's language. The work by other students of Eliot and of modernist literature generally has been similar; and it so augments Professor Melchiori's evidence that any proper consideration of the relationship between *Ulysses* and *The Waste Land* must begin with "the influence which Mr. Joyce's book may have" on Eliot's own poem.

Although in these studies the locutions "brings to mind" and "like" occur often, influence usually is claimed more positively. Some allegations are on tenuous grounds at best. For example, can Stephen's walking on the sand at Sandymount really have inspired "Sweat is dry and feet are in the sand"? Or, his "My teeth are very bad," Eliot's "Dead mountain mouth of carious teeth that cannot spit"?[30] On a more general level, one critic suggests that Eliot was "moved" by the "great achievement" of Molly's soliloquy to write the passage of the cockneys in the pub that concludes "A Game of Chess": "He must have wanted to write a comparable dramatization of the popular mind."[31] Judging from Virginia Woolf's report, Eliot would have been more inhibited than inspired by Molly's soliloquy; but in any case we now have the poet's private assertion that the passage was "stolen" from the Eliots' maid.[32] Apparently, he had the genius to incorporate a maid's anecdote in his poem and to transmute it into fine dramatic verse.

But appropriations from *Ulysses* there are nevertheless. And the problem of what to make of them is a nagging one, despite the bravado of Eliot's declaration in the Masssinger essay and his practice of incorporating lines and phrases from other works. The recently published drafts of *The Waste Land* bear two comments by Pound to the effect that passages recalled *Ulysses*; and although in the first case Pound's inference is more evidence of the effect the novel had had on him than of the effect it had had on Eliot, Eliot's sensitivity about the matter and his attitude toward it can be illustrated by the fact that in response to Pound's other comment, "*Penelope* J.J.," beside "Those are pearls that were his eyes, yes!," Eliot removed the "yes."[33] Was that "yes," in the words of his Massinger essay: "an echo, rather than an imitation or a plagiarism—the basest, because least conscious form of borrowing"?[34] Is consciousness the important issue? Moreover, regarding that very issue of his possible awareness of any specific words or other elements from *Ulysses* in his poem: unless the appropriation plainly alludes to its source in the novel, although one man's opinion is not as good as another's, there is still no way of knowing what the case happens to be. And more important is the question whether such an element is truly "stolen" in his terms or merely derivative, consciously or not.

Quite often it is impossible to make any real determination of influence because both works are so extensively allusive. Thus, although Joyce has fox and dog disinterring, and later capitalizes "Dog," Eliot attaches to line 74, where he uses "Dog," a note: "Cf. the dirge in Webster's *White Devil*." To one of Vittoria Corombona's brothers over the corpse of the other their mother recites a dirge calling on birds to bury a "friendless" body with leaves and flowers, and on small boring animals:

> To rear him hillocks that shall keep him warm,
> And (when gay tombs are robbed) sustain no harm:
> But keep the wolf far thence that's foe to men,
> For with his nails he'll dig them up again.[35]

An unmarked grave of flowers and hillocks in Webster, and a corpse buried in a garden in Eliot. Surely the dirge exploited allusively in the close paraphrase of its final couplet and the identifying note also influenced the poem. However, was *Ulysses* the direct influence? That is, did *Ulysses* move Eliot to "steal" a couplet and be influenced by other elements from an already familiar dramatic sequence, by recalling it to him? Perhaps. But Eliot's unpublished poem "The Death of the Duchess," which contributed to *The Waste Land* and is included in the drafts, is clearly based on an incident in *The Duchess of Malfi* and incorporates lines from that play and lines about "the dead" from *The White Devil*; and one remembers that the first two stanzas of a poem in his 1920 volume *Poems* (*Ara Vos Prec* in England), "Whispers of Immortality," are devoted to the subject stated in its opening line: "Webster was much possessed by death." His memory would not seem to have needed much prodding.

The question is complicated by the possibility that the scene in *The White Devil* also is behind the fox-dog material in the second and third chapters of *Ulysses*. For the fox "burying" his "grandmother" listens for and hears "bells in Heaven," and the bereaved mother introduces the dirge with: "I'll give you a saying which my grandmother was wont, when she heard the bell toll, to sing o'er unto her lute."[36] Joyce was less interested in Webster than Eliot, and the bell in *The White Devil* is a funeral bell. Nevertheless, the play may have influenced, with Joyce's awareness or otherwise, Eliot's possible source in those two chapters of his novel, and/or been construed by Eliot as having done so.

In the light of all this, how fix—beyond the punning device of the capitalized "Dog"—Eliot's indebtedness to *Ulysses* itself?

Even where a third work is not involved, attributions of indebtedness to *Ulysses* can be treacherous. To illustrate, I offer a characteristic but hitherto disregarded case of apparent influence, chosen, for the sake of consistency, from the third chapter. At a crucial point, *The Waste Land* reads:

> At the violet hour . . .
> . . . .
> I Tiresias, though blind, throbbing between two lives,

> Old man with wrinkled female breasts, can see
> At the violet hour, the evening hour . . . .

And in *Ulysses*:

> Me sits there with his augur's rod of ash, in borrowed sandals, by day
> beside a livid sea, unbeheld, in violet night walking . . . .[37]

Stephen is speaking and he says he has an augur's rod and is wearing
sandals; that could hardly be much closer to "I Tiresias." But is Joyce's
passage invoked in the poem? Certainly not to any purpose. Therefore, the
similarity either is the work of accident—an agency not admitted to the
universe of influence—or is an unconscious borrowing. The striking conjunction of Joyce's "violet night" and Eliot's "the violet hour, the evening
hour" seems to settle the issue: the literary editor of the *Egoist* stole from
the third chapter of *Ulysses* the vehicle of a good metaphor—truly "stole"
it, in his sense—and in the process "basely" caused his poem to "echo" the
context in which he found it.

Once again, the plot thickens; for the apparently stolen vehicle can be
shown to have been owned by Eliot all along. The four poems that begin
his first volume, *Prufrock and Other Observations* (1917), the first poems
published since his student years, all appeared initially in 1915. And the
situation of an evening or night walker in the city which dominates the
fourth, "Rhapsody on a Windy Night," comes up in the other three as well.
There is an untitled holograph poem or fragment among the *Waste Land*
drafts which also is dominated by that situation so pervasive in Eliot's
early poems (and metamorphosed in *The Waste Land*). It is strongly reminiscent of "Rhapsody on a Windy Night," and may even be the source
for the beginning and ending of "Prufrock." Not surprisingly, Valerie Eliot
dates this "first draft," as she calls it, "about 1914 or even earlier" from
the handwriting, and cites Conrad Aiken for confirmation.[38]

The weight of evidence is that the poem or fragment antedates Joyce's
completion of the first chapters of *Ulysses* by at least two years.[39] And,
in both cases using "violet" as a metaphor precisely for evening, not night,
it begins: "So through the evening, through the violet air . . ." and has for
its tenth line: "Oh, through the violet sky, through the evening air."

Once again it is possible that *Ulysses* served as an immediate influence:
perhaps the passage in the third chapter invoked for *The Waste Land* a
metaphor Eliot had used earlier, by recalling to him his "first draft." If so,

Ulysses also was the immediate cause of his deriving from this earlier work a stanza in the last section of his new poem (lines 378-85). And if so, other similarities between Stephen on the beach and Tiresias may well be the unconscious and gratuitous result of influence. Once again: perhaps. For it seems no more likely that Eliot needed to be reminded of his own poetry than that he needed to be reminded of a poem for the dead in Webster.

My purpose in tracing at such length the ambiguous and tenuous grounds for determining influence of the kind often adduced is to suggest that usually such influence is not important even when it happens to be true, or the indebtedness would be firm and clear. The exceptions to this are a few similar details to which students of influence have drawn attention, such as the digging "Dog." The pun was indeed "stolen," and Eliot's firm clear indebtedness is important because of the freight of meaning he carried over from *Ulysses* with it. In the same sense, although the case has been overlooked, he probably did steal Joyce's thunder. I have tried to demonstrate elsewhere that in the fourteenth chapter of *Ulysses* Joyce contrives to assert: that Bloom can achieve his salvation only by acting in emulation of the one true father in the novel, Theodore Purefoy—pure of faith; and that Stephen can do so only by submitting his will to God—as Odysseus's companions would have been saved had they shown reverence for the god of the sacred cattle of fertility. Joyce's assertion about his characters' diverse ways to salvation is punctuated by thunder and a fructifying rainstorm.[40] In "What the Thunder Said," much the same thing happens.

Eliot "stole" from the novel in progress that he so admired, as he stole from other sources; and perhaps he did "imitate" and even occasionally "echo" Joyce in places. But any such indebtedness is of minor importance in the relationship between *Ulysses* and *The Waste Land*. The grander, the truly significant similarities between them seem to me not a matter of influence, but rather, with one exception, a matter of profound modernist confluence.

That exception is the fact of a pattern of allusion informing *The Waste Land* and having for referent an ancient myth. There can be no certainty about the history of its development until all manuscripts and notebooks are available, if then; but the extant drafts of Eliot's poem indicate a major debt to Joyce's novel.

They also record the apparent evolution of that debt. The process of eliciting from them an empirically sound account is a complicated one, but necessary. Distinguishing adequately those similarities between *Ulysses* and *The Waste Land* which are the result of influence requires that the one significant influence of *Ulysses* be confirmed. The remainder of this section is an endeavor to confirm it by demonstrating its evolution from the drafts.

Some elements of *The Waste Land* antedate *Ulysses* by as much as the earliest poems and fragments included with the drafts and related to it, such as the "first draft" of about 1914 and "The Death of Saint Narcissus," which may be earlier still.[41] But even had he been acquainted with Joyce's use of the *Odyssey* before he put down a line, Eliot would not have followed suit. At one stage the first two sections of what he habitually alluded to as "a long poem" had the general title "He do the Police in Different Voices" (the source is Betty Higden's praise of Sloppy's mimicry as he reads aloud from a newspaper such as the then popular *People's Police Gazette* in Dickens's *Our Mutual Friend,* Book the First, chapter xvi). One obvious inference from the different title he gave the "long poem" he was writing is that when he drafted those two sections his conception of it did not warrant its being called "The Waste Land."

Once this inference has been formulated, the evidence supporting it seems incontrovertible. Hugh Kenner argues cogently and convincingly that the poem Eliot actually began to create was a neo-Augustan urban satire.[42] And the drafts reveal enough of what was excised and what was added later to show that in any case it was not *The Waste Land*. Wasteland and Grail references were appropriate for direct and ironic treatment of Eliot's "unreal city" from the start, and some do appear in the early stages of composition; but although he marshalled them to serve his ultimate conception once he evolved it, initially he employed these references for other purposes: for example, to contrast false with true spiritual wisdom (Madame Sosostris and Tiresias), or to suggest death and salvation (the "fishing" prince Ferdinand from *The Tempest*). Even so apparently pointed an element as the drought passage in "The Burial of the Dead" (lines 19-30) derives in part from "The Death of Saint Narcissus," is related explicitly to *Ezekiel*, and has echoes of *Isaiah*.[43]

If the poem was "written, mostly when I was at Lausanne" (between late November 1921 and early the next January), the original version of the third section, "The Fire Sermon"—which had a long opening passage not in *The Waste Land* and ended abruptly a few lines after the typist sequence—apparently was not. Three machines were used to type the drafts of the five sections. The last two sections were typed on Pound's machine; the first two were done on a different machine; and only the third was typed, in its original version, on the machine also used for the title page and, the following October, for the shipping label that directed the draft material (the subject of the facsimile edition) from Eliot's home address in London to John Quinn.[44] This would appear to be a standard machine that Eliot used when at home, not only from the evidence of the label but also because the title page most probably was typed after his return from Lausanne with the drafts of the poem in his luggage. In the famous exchange of letters following Eliot's return, Pound mentions the (temporary) epigraph from Conrad's "Heart of Darkness" on the title page as though it is new to him.[45] And this chronology for the title page is confirmed internally by the fact that the title eventually typed on it had a provisional predecessor that headed the first two sections and was abandoned before the fourth section was written out in a fair copy—that is, was abandoned while Eliot was away from home.

We must conclude that "The Fire Sermon" was typed before the last two sections because these were typed on Pound's machine in Paris, where Eliot visited him during the Lausanne trip, and because we know from the drafts that Pound and Eliot worked over "The Fire Sermon" more than any other section, a number of times, and in typed form.[46] And, because it was typed on the machine Eliot used later in London for the title page and the shipping label, it apparently was typed in London. If the first two sections also were typed (on a different machine) in London, how much of the poem was in fact "written . . . at Lausanne"? And why was the other machine used to type them?[47] "The Fire Sermon" may antedate the rest of the poem considerably, since it was in the previous May that Eliot had written to Quinn of "a long poem" as "partly on paper"; or he may have composed it at "Margate Sands" and typed it up during the week he spent in London between his month at Margate and his departure for Lausanne. In any case the evidence indicates that he left London for Lausanne with the typed draft of "The Fire Sermon," and that it was composed before Part I and Part II of "He do the Police in Different Voices."[48] Thus, the typed draft not only fails to bear that general title but is not numbered, although the holograph fair copy of "Death by Water" in Eliot's hand is also headed "Part IV."[49]

The probable initial composition of the original "Fire Sermon" is important because that priority combines with the absence of a "part" number designation, with the extensive editing by Pound and revising and cutting by Eliot, and above all with Eliot's eventual additions to it, to confirm that it was not composed for its ultimate role in Eliot's ultimate poem. Then, so late in the genesis of that poem that no typed or even fair holograph copy of the passage is included in the drafts, so late that it bears no evidence of having been seen by Pound, Eliot wrote in pencil, on the back of the mock-Augustan opening of "The Fire Sermon" portraying Fresca at her morning toilet, a rough draft of ten lines. Those rough pencilled lines—after the substitution of "silk handkerchiefs" for "newspapers" at the beginning of the sixth, the elimination of "and" in two places, and the filling out of the truncated allusions "Sweet Thames etc." and "by the waters"—replaced the seventy original lines of heroic couplets to begin "III. The Fire Sermon" of *The Waste Land:*

> The rivers [sic] tent is broken and [sic]
>   the last fingers of leaf
> Clutch and sink into the wet bank. The wind
> Crosses the brown land, unheard. . . .[50]

Correspondingly, on three separate sheets of paper, only one of which bears comments by Pound, Eliot pencilled the draft of the last forty-five lines of the section, beginning:

> The river sweats
> Oil and tar
> . . . .[51]

Corrupted water, *Götterdämmerung, Inferno,* the pilgrim Saint Augustine: and again the rough pencilled passage is almost word for word what was published.

The very last lines of "The Fire Sermon" are implied in its title, and it is possible that Eliot had them and much else of his new last third (almost exactly one-third) of the section in mind for some time. But that cannot be the case with the ten lines for whose clear suggestion of drought and a waste land he decisively employed the back of the ribbon copy of the original opening lines.

Although he was not moved to make additions implementing the wasteland theme to the draft of either "The Burial of the Dead" or "A Game of Chess," "The Fire Sermon" of Eliot's original poem was drastically altered to function in a new one, and altered with a sure hand. Furthermore, that new poem seems to have evolved late. Both the first two sections antedate the rough and mostly unedited pencilled passages in "The Fire Sermon," as their typed state and the extensive revisions made to them attest. And this clear evidence of a late conceptualization of what he was about, or wished to be about, in his poem is confirmed and further clarified by the last two sections, the eventual title, and the Notes.

Of the draft of the fourth section only a small fraction, the last tenth (lines 84-93), was published as "IV. Death by Water" of *The Waste Land*. And the excision of the major part of the draft version was done neither on Eliot's holograph copy nor on the typed copy edited (extensively) by Pound. In other words, the final state of the section was evolved at least as late as were the unique wasteland additions to "The Fire Sermon," for it is not in the drafts at all; probably it was first recorded in the lost nineteen-page fair copy of the poem mentioned by Pound, in his letter commenting to Eliot on the new title page, and elsewhere.[52]

The final state of "V. What the Thunder Said" is, by dramatic contrast, almost word for word as Eliot wrote the whole section in pencil in rough draft—precisely as is the case with the rough pencilled additions to "The Fire Sermon." And that fact about "What the Thunder Said" further confirms what had happened in the genesis of the poem. But it does considerably more. It combines with the very different history of the drastically modified section just before "What the Thunder Said" to fix the point at which Eliot conceived what he was about—contracted his debt to *Ulysses*—and *The Waste Land* evolved. A drama, in which a suddenly manifest influence generated or catalyzed creative inspiration, is immanent in the *Waste Land* drafts. And the key to that drama is the rough pencilled draft of "What the Thunder Said."

The typed pages that precede "What the Thunder Said" in "a long poem" and were worked over by Pound have a total of 511 lines; exactly half that draft material, 255 lines and two half-lines, was included in or adapted to *The Waste Land*. Of the rejected 255 lines, 252 came from four places. Forty-four lines and two half-lines were edited out of the Smyrna merchant and typist sequences in "The Fire Sermon" by Pound or under his direction. The other passages were not revised and pruned but simply excluded from *The Waste Land*: of the two parts of "He do the Police in Different Voices," "The Burial of the Dead" begins with fifty-four lines about a night on the town (apparently Boston); the Fresca passage at the beginning of "The Fire Sermon" is seventy lines; the excised first part of "Death by Water" is an eighty-three-line introduction and narrative of a fishing voyage to the Grand Banks. Eliot declared that Pound "induced me to destroy" the Fresca passage because of the quality of the verse, and

Pound edited it more heavily than he did the excised part of "Death by Water." Even if Eliot simply responded to Pound's judgment in that case, we do not know why, or when, he excluded the opening passage of the first section; and we do know that he reduced "Death by Water" to one-tenth its size after Pound had expended a good deal of effort working over the rejected nine-tenths.

By this point it should be manifest that the poem from which those three long passages were excluded, in which were printed almost word-for-word the rough pencilled parts of "The Fire Sermon" and draft of "What the Thunder Said," and which incorporated a set of pointedly allusive notes and the title *The Waste Land*, was the product of an inspiration both late and clear. When Eliot's inspiration came he could decide to just cut away from the fourth section of his poem in process, if before his inspiration not surely in progress, the nine-tenths which "il miglior fabbro," until his inspiration his arbiter, even co-creator, had shaped down so laboriously in typescript.

That radical excision, like the Notes, the title, and three at least of the four and a half rough pencilled sheets for "The Fire Sermon" which were not put into typed or even fair holograph form in the drafts, belongs to the denouement of the drama. Its prologue is Eliot's composition of the fourth section of "a long poem."

Eliot's declaration that *The Waste Land* was written "mostly . . . at Lausanne" discourages speculation that the original long version of "Death by Water" may have been seen by Pound when Eliot passed through Paris on his way *to* Lausanne, and perhaps even typed on Pound's machine at that time and left there for Pound to "attack," as he put it beside the opening lines of the (fair) holograph copy: "Bad—but can't attack until I get typescript." As a consequence, it must be assumed that the typing of both the last two sections of the poem was done during Eliot's visit to Pound when returning to London from Lausanne. However, that they were typed *at the same time* during Eliot's visit does not necessarily follow.

Pound read, for he commented briefly at the head of, the holograph draft of each of those two sections. The roughness of the draft of "What the Thunder Said" indicates that Eliot had had no chance to make a fair holograph copy to show to Pound, as he had done in the case of "Death by Water." The logical inference to draw from this is that Eliot experienced his crucial inspiration and created his virtually final rough draft of "What the Thunder Said" either during his visit or so little time before as to prevent recopying—not to mention typing—it before he set out for Paris.

The fulfillment of his inspiration included his evolution of "The Fire Sermon" of *The Waste Land* with the four and a half sheets of virtually final rough draft. Eliot's composition and employment of those pencilled sheets can now be considered in context.

One and one-half sheets had been composed already. The half-sheet has what became lines 259-65 written *above* the rough draft of a passage typed up in the original "Fire Sermon": therefore, those lines were composed early and set aside (see n. 51). The one sheet, a draft of the quatrain spoken by the woman seduced in a canoe and the quatrain following that one, bears Pound's comments "O.K." and "echt"; and "Type out this *anyhow*" is beside a cancelled pair of stanzas that are earlier versions: therefore, he saw the sheet twice. Because he did not comment on the remaining three sheets or on the half sheet, it seems reasonable to conclude that he did not see them. (The quatrains on the sheet Eliot showed him twice are coherent read in isolation, and they fitted readily between the contents of the other two pencilled sheets at the end of "The Fire Sermon.") A second reasonable conclusion is that none of the sheets were typed up because Eliot had not decided to use their contents in his "long poem" before the last material which was put into typed form, the pencilled draft of "What the Thunder Said," had been typed in Paris on Pound's machine. Finally, there is no evidence that the material on the three full sheets neither commented on by Pound nor typed up was in existence before then. As was said, the key to the drama is that rough pencilled draft.

The roughness of the draft makes likely not only that Eliot composed it just before or after his arrival in Paris, but also that he would have typed it up himself; and the state of the typescript indicates that indeed he did type it. Silent stylistic changes made during typing (such as those to lines 326 and 370), and other details like the reversal of an earlier choice among two phrases (in line 339), would seem to be the work of the one who composed the lines.

Furthermore, the state of the typescript indicates that Pound did not work on it when he worked on the typescripts of the first four sections of the poem. Unless every occasion on which he saw the two copies of that of the original "Fire Sermon" was earlier, he "attacked" the typescripts of all four sections during Eliot's visit, the first three having arrived "in [Eliot's] suitcase," and that of "Death by Water" having been produced to his order. His letter about the poem which comments on the title page included in the drafts apparently is a covering letter, for it begins "Caro mio: MUCH improved"; and he could have first seen the typescript of "What the Thunder Said" when Eliot sent it as part of the nineteen-page text the letter refers to. But even if Eliot did show it to him before leaving Paris, the difference between his treatment of it and his previous slashing flamboyance is eloquent. He corrected three typographical errors (and compounded a fourth); he neatly circled elements he questioned; and he suggested very minor changes in a discreet hand: the elimination of three words and two cases of plural s, and the alteration of a phrase. The three words, two instances of "the" in a line and a single adjective, "black" (cock), were excised; the plurals remained; and Eliot made his own change to the phrase. The poet had become confident, the editor newly respectful of the poet's creation and assisting in the polishing of a completed poem (the first sentence of the final paragraph in Pound's covering letter is "Complimenti, you bitch").

This extremely detailed review of the evidence in the drafts enables a reconstruction of the drama of influence made manifest in sudden creative inspiration. It occurred at that point in the history of *The Waste Land* when Eliot created the last element of the poem for which he made a typed draft. And probably he created "What the Thunder Said" before he created crucial portions of "The Fire Sermon" not seen by Pound which appear in the drafts on three rough pencilled sheets and in virtually their published state.

He created "What the Thunder Said" either just before or during the "few days" he spent with Pound. If the former is the case, he showed Pound the pair of quatrains in "The Fire Sermon," the fair copy of "Death by Water" and the just-completed rough draft of "What the Thunder Said"; Pound wrote general comments on them and returned them; and using Pound's machine he typed up the draft of "Death by Water" (for example, in the typescript "northern seas," rejected for "eastern banks" in the holograph draft, is restored) that Pound wanted to "get" for working over, then typed up "What the Thunder Said."

The more dramatic latter alternative is also the more likely one—that Eliot arrived in Paris with the fair holograph copy of "Death by Water," but did not experience his inspiration and produce his virtually final draft of "What the Thunder Said" until after his arrival, conceived and wrote it during the time Pound was working over the typescripts of the first four sections; and he showed his new work in that state to Pound. He also showed Pound the pair of quatrains newly revised from the earlier stanzas, which Pound had seen and suggested his typing up "anyway" shortly after his arrival. Thus, Pound pronounced the quatrains "O.K." and "echt" in green crayon; and at the head of "What the Thunder Said" Pound also— and also in green crayon—wrote "OK."

This scenario of the drama is the more likely one for at least three reasons. To begin with, that Pound read the rough draft of "What the Thunder Said" instead of waiting a bit for a more legible text suggests that Eliot typed it up late in his visit rather than at the time he produced the typescript of "Death by Water." Furthermore, while the first two sections of the original "long poem" were typed at Lausanne (see n. 47), "Death by Water" was not. This suggests that Eliot in fact wrote *that* section just before his departure and made the fair holograph copy during the journey from Lausanne to Paris; and at least some of the hundred thirteen lines of "What the Thunder Said" could have been recopied then as well, if they existed (indeed, the journey should have afforded more than enough time to recopy all). Finally, that Eliot did not decide to eliminate from *The Waste Land* the major part of "Death by Water" during the time Pound was working on it, or even before his departure from Paris, also points to those "few days" as the time of Eliot's initial dramatic inspiration.

Perhaps just before but probably during his stay in Paris, as though in a creative burst, he crystallized with rapidly pencilled lines his motifs of sterility, despair, quest and salvation, and provided the chapel perilous, the holy river, the voice of God in the thunder. Perhaps as an afterthought Pound wrote in ink beside that green "OK": "OK from here on *I think.*" After completing the original versions of four sections of his poem Eliot had found his way; and Pound the superb critic knew it.

Eliot typed up "What the Thunder Said," departed for home and there composed the poem we know as *The Waste Land* out of the drafts of "a long poem" by the light of the new inspiration that had produced "What the Thunder Said" in virtually its printed state with such remarkable certainty. With the same sure hand he: provided elements first mentioned by Pound in the famous exchange of letters, such as the drastically abbreviated final "Death by Water'" and the explicit mythic title itself; restored the seven early lines set aside; wrote out a page of pencilled lines of the corrupt Thames to connect the seven lines to the two quatrains and added those; added another page of despair to end "The Fire Sermon"; and on the verso of its original first page added a third page of pencilled lines to begin it. (Perhaps not before he did these things following his return home did he excise the original beginning of "The Burial of the

Dead," that of "The Fire Sermon," or both.) Finally, like the published form of "Death by Water" and a few connecting lines and minor revisions not represented in the drafts—apparently not even in the nineteen-page text of the poem with title seen by Pound—came the Notes, with their long expository headnote citing Jessie Weston's book, Frazer, dying and resurrected gods, the Grail legend and so on.

Though Pound's ultimate mark on *The Waste Land* is a notable event in literary history, it is actually less great than his mark on the drafts of the poem. The exchange of letters records his continuing criticism and advice; but Eliot essentially had pried the poem away from him, taken full possession of it, using for lever another influence.

To quote the title of Eliot's essay, his poem, like *Ulysses*, would derive "order" from "myth," achieve its coherence and express its meaning principally by way of a pattern of allusions to a specific ancient myth. The myth scarcely could be that of Homer's Achaean father, hero and husband. But the Weston book was a scholarly work (however brilliantly syncretic) whose existence was devoted to the Grail material Eliot himself eventually exploited as a resource for his own work of art; it "suggested," as his head note says, the "title . . . the plan and . . . incidental symbolism," but not the uses to which they could be put. And years before its publication in 1922, Eliot began to be thoroughly familiar with and admire *Ulysses*, a novel which was exploiting myth to provide a new resource for art. When these facts are set beside the considerable internal evidence of the evolution of *The Waste Land*, and set beside his statements about the importance of *Ulysses* and the pioneer significance for other writers of Joyce's "using . . . the mythical method" in it, a grand and fundamental influence seems fairly certain.

4

MULTUM ET PARVUM

The question, then, about Mr. Joyce, is: how much living material does he deal with, and how does he deal with it . . . ?

In a characteristically rich section of her study of Eliot's poetry, Dame Helen Gardner says calmly of *The Waste Land* and *Ulysses*, "The two works have much in common," alludes to the use of an ordering myth in each, and goes beyond the readily apparent:

> The exploration of the past of the human race and of the depths of the human soul . . . appears . . . as a method . . . . Both works are visions of a city . . . . Both combine within a single work an extraordinary variety of styles . . . . Both are richly allusive . . . . Both works again juxtapose boldly a modern world described with the most complete realism, and a world of romance, epic and high tragedy.[53]

And this level of comparison is the necessary one if what the novel and the poem have to reveal about each other and about Modernism is to be elicited. Dame Helen is chiefly concerned, though, with "fundamentally different attitudes" she says inform the two works.

I have been criticized for trying to demonstrate that *Ulysses* is a religious novel, literally,[54] and will not do so at this point; I only will declare my inability to agree that it is "without God," as Dame Helen says, for the evidence of the narrative seems to me to assert the exact opposite. Yet the "fundamentally different attitudes to life" that she finds in the works are in a certain sense there, and are suggested by the different histories of their composition. The process of excision and compression engaged in by Eliot (and Pound) was long well known and recently documented; Eliot's late inspiration precipitated its most fruitful phase. Generally known only to students of Joyce's work is the fact that in that respect *Ulysses* underwent an equally unusual, and precisely the opposite, development. There were constant expansions in the manuscript, then in the typescript; then the proofs were added to and reset through a total of five successive sets of proof. There were even frantic trips to the printer in Dijon so that "revisions" (as Joyce usually called his expansions) could be made in press. What was accomplished above all was a thickening, principally in the case of Bloom, of the web of internal associations by which the novel so largely works. For *Ulysses* was not so much written as built up.

In a vulgar sense the distinction may be between the creative process and product of an artist reared as a puritan and those of an artist reared as a Catholic. The distinction is fundamentally that between an ascetic artwork and a sensual one; and the visions within the works correspond— the one revulsion at a debased world and hope for transcendence through the spirit, the other an embracing of created life. Eliot's conversion of Joyce's dog motif, discussed above, exemplifies the contrast of visions; so presumably does the fact that his percipient and sympathetic critic Dame Helen refers to the chapter of *Ulysses* before Molly's robust soliloquy as "the last chapter."

These fundamental differences between *Ulysses* and *The Waste Land* cannot be stressed too much in the present context. However, they more reinforce my general argument than the opposite; for the significant similarities between those two epitomes of Modernism that cannot be explained as the result of influence exist in despite of such differences, as though they had been compelled by something that was even more fundamental to the condition of art and life fifty years ago.

5

THE "METHOD"

In using the myth, in manipulating a continuous parallel between contemporaneity and antiquity, Mr. Joyce is pursuing a method which others must pursue after him. It is simply a way of controlling, of ordering, of giving a shape and a significance to the immense panorama of futility and anarchy which is contemporary history. It is a method already adumbrated by Mr. Yeats, and of the need for which I believe Mr. Yeats to have been the first contemporary to be conscious. It is a method for which the horoscope is auspicious. . . . Instead of narrative method, we may now use the mythical method. It is, I seriously believe, a step toward making the modern world possible for art . . . .

Yeats did not share Eliot's view of a kinship between them with respect to "the mythical method": three years later, in the first edition of *A Vision*, he explicitly criticized *Ulysses* and *The Waste Land* for their "using the myth" and their common allusive strategy as a whole.[55] Eliot's statement needs additional qualification. Although he represents *Ulysses* as exploiting a single pervading myth, that "myth" is strictly speaking a literary work. And his own practice proves his awareness that in any case the new "method" is not merely a matter of choosing an object of a particular sort for alluding to, nor even is essentially the writer's "manipulating a continuous parallel between contemporaneity and [the chosen myth out of] antiquity," as he describes it. The method, he was aware, is rather the new methodical use of allusion which *Ulysses* and *The Waste Land* have in common. Neither Yeats, who criticized them for it, nor Pound, in the *Cantos* then published, was employing that new allusive strategy. And the extent to which Joyce and Eliot did so in their novel and poem has rarely been equalled.

Although in the past the familiar literary device of alluding to elements of culture or history or other literature had provided primarily a decorative and illustrative—and therefore casual and overt—enrichment, the modernists' innovation is not their use of structurally intrinsic and pervasive patterns of allusion to accomplish important tasks of exposition or thematic statement. In Dante's *Commedia,* Herbert's *The Temple*, certain "imitations" of classical poems in the Renaissance and later, Dryden's *Absalom and Achitophel, Candide,* and a number of other earlier works that could be cited in their place, the relationships created between the alluding work and the objects of allusion vary, and so do the functions which allusion is given; but unvaryingly it is intrinsic and/or pervasive, and it accomplishes important tasks. The difference exemplified by *Ulysses* and *The Waste Land* lies in their extension of what earlier works had done with both the allusive relationship and the task allotted to allusion, a new modernist conception of formal and functional possibilities.

The earlier practice was to set up in a work or section of a long work a relationship with a single object of allusion. This was not the case with a burlesque, which would parody more than one example of a genre to satirize it effectively; but burlesque actually is a means of commentary on the objects of allusion, not a use of them for autonomous ends, and so is exceptional. Still, even burlesques as comprehensive as the first part of *Don Quixote* and Buckingham's *The Rehearsal* do not equal the montages of allusive bits and pieces that Joyce and Eliot created in *Ulysses* and *The Waste Land*; and the range of different types of sources in each work is totally unprecedented.

More audacious than their extension of earlier practice in this respect is the second development in the two works: the task Joyce and Eliot allotted to allusion. In earlier literature and drama in which allusion has an intrinsic and vital function, that function is to enhance an already coherent and complete literal discourse or action. This is so even if the augmentation or enrichment of meaning provided by the allusive presence, its own signification, eclipses in importance the bare literal entity. Allusion so enhances effect and meaning in *Ulysses* and *The Waste Land* as well, but on some occasions it has a more fundamental task. Neither work was given a coherent complete literal discourse or action. Rather, the very proceeding in both often is by way of the allusive referents of the words as much as by way of their lexical referents; in both works sense and integrity depend upon contributions made by various objects of allusion. The eventual means by which Eliot won his struggle to achieve an articulate and coherent poem is a vivid illustration of this fact; nor can one conceive of an articulate and coherent narrative of the stories of Bloom and Stephen shorn of the allusions in *Ulysses*.

More than anything else, this second special use of allusion by certain modernist writers makes it in the fullest sense a "method"—in Joyce's words, a "way of working": when asked by a French critic why he "followed the pattern of the Odyssey" in *Ulysses* he had replied, "Everyone has his own way of working."[56] And although others (and Eliot after 1922) were less systematic in their use of it, Joyce was to employ the "method" almost totally in *Finnegans Wake*. For example, both portmanteau words and multilingual puns refer the reader to elements of language itself rather than to those things beyond language that are the normal referents of language; that is, they allude to *other words* (in order to invoke the referents of those words).

The extent of quotation from Eliot's essay at the head of this section is an attempt to provide evidence of the importance he was then attaching to the "method" and of the reasons why that was the case. There had been a "need" for it; it was a response to the nature of the reality faced by him and his contemporaries. Perhaps it enabled the assertion of continuity in art, culture and society at a time of acute confrontation with the very opposite; for a "way of working" that by its very nature linked present human experience with the past was "a way of . . . giving a shape and a significance to the immense panorama of futility and anarchy which is contemporary history" and so a means for "making the modern world possible for art."

No single novel or poem could be nearly exemplary of all modernist literature, even in its own genre and language. That fact bears repeating. But the ascetic poem and the sensual novel published in 1922 operate in similar ways; furthermore, they do so to achieve a number of similar ends; and they even express similar views of the world in which they were made, similar views of art, and similar views of the relationship of art not only to that world but even to the artist himself. It is through the articulation of this rich cluster of similarities, similarities of artistic practice, thematic concern and conception of art and the artist—a matter of confluence more often than influence, and unimpeded by the difference in composition and outlook of the two works—that their complementary reputations can be understood and can cast some light on the nature of Modernism.

Those other elements in the cluster of similarities which are manifestations of the method at work attest to the extent of Joyce's and Eliot's reliance on it. When in the third chapter of *Ulysses* Stephen is likened to Menelaus, the allusion is invoked principally by his thinking of Mananaan MacLir, the mythical Irish Celtic equivalent to Proteus. The Grail legend and that of Tristram and Iseult also are Celtic; and, as I shall try to show, the myth of Odysseus is used (*used* is the proper term) in Eliot's poem along with its other Hellenic material. Both novel and poem use the Germanic myth of the *Götterdämmerung*. And both use the Hebraic and Christian myths of salvation based on the prophets and Jesus. Correspondingly, both use the works in which these myths are embodied, or have been represented: the Bible, the *Odyssey*, the *Commedia* of Dante, Wagner's Ring cycle. These striking specific coincidences are not just accident. In addition both use Shakespeare, and each uses a number of other artifacts of European high culture. For example, the novel uses the *Arabian Nights*, a work by Bishop Fuller, Goethe's *Faust, Don Giovanni*, a whole series of English prose works such as *Pilgrim's Progress* and *A Tale of a Tub*, and poems by Irish poets ranging in time from Thomas Moore to Yeats. The poem uses Vergil, Ovid, Saint Augustine, Chaucer, Kyd, Spenser, Webster, Marvell, Goldsmith, Baudelaire, Gérard de Nerval and Verlaine.

In both works, the allusive method also uses elements of popular culture. Though *The Waste Land* as published uses only the Shakespeherian rag and the song of Sweeney and Mrs. Porter (in one version of that song it is not her feet that young Miss Porter washes), the original drafts contain an extensive use of American popular songs of the time. *Ulysses* uses a highly popular sentimental novel, a popular pornographic novel, a sentimental opera, current newspapers, and many street ballads, popular songs, and folk and art songs sung in Dublin in 1904.

Allusive invocation of myths of major branches of our civilization, and of classic artifacts of high culture and characteristic artifacts of popular culture (augmented by references to various philosophers and specific historical figures in the two works), begins to accomplish by collective action a general and thematic purpose which is additional to the specific and technical purpose of moving the work forward that is accomplished by each particular incorporated phrase, or by the particular invocation of the source or context of that phrase. The groups of myths, masterworks and the rest conjoin to represent a civilization in its stages—Hebraic, Hellenic, medieval, renaissance, modern.

The common thematic purpose of the two modernist writers can best be indicated by way of one of their important common sources—a poet to whom Joyce was devoted, according to his biographers, and who, according to Eliot's poetry, criticism and testimony, had "the most persistent and deepest influence" on him.[57] Eventually, Eliot placed Dante at the very beginning of *The Waste Land*, dedicating the poem to Pound with a phrase Dante had used for Arnaut Daniel. The phrase is from the *Purgatorio*, from an earlier part of which Eliot incorporates a line at the end of his poem, significantly a suggestion (reinforced in the Notes) of Arnaut's ultimate deliverance. A corresponding allusion in *Ulysses* is more important to the novel. Shortly before he leaves it to Bloom and Molly, Stephen sings the psalm of deliverance sung at the beginning of the *Purgatorio* by the souls being brought to purgatory, a psalm described by Dante in his famous letter to Can Grande as signifying man's redemption by Christ.

But the primary reference in both works is to the first part of Dante's poem. The role of the Odysseus myth in *The Waste Land* is the role in it of Tiresias, whom the Achaean hero sought out in Hades and who told him his fate. The long fishing-voyage passage that Eliot excised from "Death by Water" he said and the evidence shows had its source not so much in Homer's epic as in the Ulysses Canto (XXVI) of Dante's *Inferno*.[58] When one recalls that Pound began his own *Cantos* with an account of the descent of the exiled hero to Hades, and that he called the nighttown chapter of *Ulysses*—in which all that has happened to them in Dublin is epitomized for Bloom and Stephen—"a new Inferno in full sail," one aspect at least of the special significance of Dante for these (and other) modernist writers becomes clear.[59] A student of Joyce has recently demonstrated the extent of his use of Dante in *Ulysses*; and she confirms Pound's perception by showing that at the beginning of the nighttown chapter Joyce presents a whole series of correspondences to Dante's entry into Hell in Canto I of the *Inferno*.[60]

The pattern of allusion to the *Inferno* in Eliot's poem needs no discussion: it all but dominates the portrayal of London in "The Burial of the Dead." The phrases "this stony rubbish" and "a heap of broken images" refer with rich effect to the poem itself, but most immediately they refer to London, refer, like a similar passage at the end of Part V of Pound's "Hugh Selwyn Mauberly":

> For two gross of broken statues
> For a few thousand battered books

to the civilization of Western man. Eliot's wasteland London is Joyce's center-of-paralysis Dublin, his city of benightedness ("nighttown" was not the name of Dublin's brothel district). And both works present visions of a desired apocalypse destroying the central artifact of man's civilization. In *Ulysses*, Stephen thinks: "I hear the ruin of all space, shattered glass and toppling masonry, and time one livid final flame"; and when he makes his climactic gesture in nighttown, in imitation of Siegfried's bringing about the *Götterdämmerung*, the phrases are repeated.[61] Just before a significant change occurs in the last part of *The Waste Land* appear the lines:

> Falling towers
> Jerusalem Athens Alexandria
> Vienna London

Hebraic, Hellenic, early Christian, renaissance, modern—Eliot's sequence, with the movement it presents westward, away from salvation and the City of God, makes my point: in their works the creators of *Ulysses* and *The Waste Land* saw fit to attempt, and by means of the commitment both made to the allusive method they achieve, similar representations of their civilization. A decade ago Lionel Trilling isolated as the "characteristic element" of modernist literature ("or at least of the most highly developed modern literature") "the bitter line of hostility to civilization which runs through it."[62] And recently Monroe K. Spears addressed himself precisely to the matter:

> For the moderns . . . the City is seen as falling . . . or as fallen . . . and therefore moving toward the Infernal City . . . . Dante and Baudelaire are the poets whose infernal visions haunt the modern writer . . . .[63]

Just as the allusive strategy works incrementally to express a view of civilization, it works in the same way to make other kinds of thematic statement. For example, *Ulysses* and *The Waste Land* have in common patterns of allusion to three specific kinds of mythic, literary and historical figures. These three common patterns are the instruments of additional significant similarities of thematic concern in the two works.

The Waste Land presents a series of males and females who are victims or victimizers, and whose relationships are characterized by failure, lust, cruelty, treachery. The ancient and mythic figures are generally more violent, the recent ones more tawdry: Actaeon and Diana; Dido and Aeneas; Philomela, Procne and Tereus; Tristram and Iseult; Antony and Cleopatra; La Pia and Nello della Pietra; Elizabeth and Leicester; Sweeney and Mrs. Porter (and her daughter); the typist and the young man carbuncular. The vision of love in *The Waste Land* corresponds to that of civilization generally. But in *Ulysses* the method makes a contrary assertion about the same concern, despite an unpromising beginning and the presence of a series of temptresses: Bloom finally becomes the Don Giovanni of Molly's Zerlina; there are Martha and Lionel of von Flotow's opera, Matcham who achieves his masterstroke with the lady in the story Bloom has read, and the Purefoys; and always in the background Odysseus is rejoining Penelope—all to present connubial love (despite some genial mocking) as an alternative to the spiritually destructive City.

A second series in each work is one of saviors, martyrs, and false and true prophets. Saviors and martyrs include: Christ in both; Moses, Robert Emmet and the "croppy boy" in *Ulysses*; and in *The Waste Land* Buddha and the dead and resurrected gods listed in the headnote. For prophets, both have Isaiah and Tiresias. To these *Ulysses* adds the Biblical figures Elijah, Elisha and Malachi; *The Waste Land*, Ezekiel and the prophet of *Ecclesiastes*. In addition to Biblical figures, *Ulysses* has Proteus, Mananaan MacLir, and the (historical) false modern prophet John Alexander Dowie; *The Waste Land* has Saint Augustine, the sybil, and the (Huxleyan) false modern prophetess, Madame Sosotris. The lists are suggestive, for they— again by an incremental pattern—assert that a certain measure of importance attaches to spiritual guides and saviors: that both novel and poem are concerned with the question of salvation from the doomed modern City.

A final group of figures express a common representation by Joyce and Eliot of what constitutes meaningful conduct for the protagonists of the two works. Up to a point (the eleventh chapter of *Ulysses* and "The Fire Sermon" respectively), Bloom, Stephen and the protagonist of *The Waste Land* are walkers in the City and doomed victims of it. Their peripatetic experiences are a means by which novel and poem both close in on the condition of modern urban man. Those experiences are accompanied by the characters' efforts to survive in things as they are, combined with nostalgia for an untroubled past condition, and with despair.

Then in both works a similar development occurs. The saviors and true prophets begin to have an effect: the characters begin to seek rescue from their predicaments. Hugh Kenner has pointed out the ironic echo of Chaucer:

> Whan that Aprille with his shoures soote
> The droghte of March hath perced to the roote
> And bathed every veyne in swich licour
> Of which vertu engendred is the flour
>
> . . . .
> Thanne longen folk to goon on pilgrimages

in Eliot's own opening lines:

> April is the cruellest month, breeding
> Lilacs out of the dead land, mixing
> Memory and desire, stirring
> Dull roots with spring rain.[64]

But the passage is fully allusive, specifically invoking the corresponding opening lines of the *Canterbury Tales*; for the most significant irony is that Eliot's protagonist ultimately goes on a pilgrimage.

A measure of what happens in the poem is the changing relationship of the "memory and desire"—active yearning—that April has mixed in the protagonist. Like his counterparts in *Ulysses*, for whom in its early chapters memory is equally prominent, he feels trapped and despairs until his desire causes him to seek rescue. In "The Burial of the Dead" his consciousness is largely occupied by memories out of the past: the Starnbergersee, the Hyacinth garden, Madame Sosostris, what he said to Stetson. In "A Game of Chess," his mostly silent exchange with the first woman and witness to the anecdote of the second both bring the past into the present of his despairing consciousness; however, the emphasis on portrayal of the women, who are linked respectively to the idle and depraved simultaneous actions in Middleton's *Women Beware Women*, still strongly suggests the urban satire out of which the poem apparently evolved. In "The Fire Sermon," the significant change occurs: alongside static memories, which merely reinforce his despair, the protagonist actively experiences in the present. Eliot's disposition of the two elements attests nicely to his conversion of the original "Fire Sermon" to its ultimate role in his ultimate poem. The protagonist remembers meeting Stetson in the "Unreal City, / Under the brown fog of a winter dawn," in "The Burial of the Dead"; and in "The Fire Sermon" the same lines, with the last word altered to "noon," are attached to his memory of Mr. Eugenides. Also, there are his memories of fishing in the polluted canal, and of the Philomela depiction in the sitting room of the first woman in "A Game of Chess." On the other hand, in the lines of Eliot's late inspiration with which "The Fire Sermon" begins, the protagonist gives extended expression to the despair he is experiencing; and in those with which it ends, he speaks of his purgative suffering and his belief that the Lord is "plucking" him "out." (Both the seduced women and Tiresias actually are in the protagonist's present experience: the women merely talk of the past, and the prophet says that he foreknew what is currently happening.) "Death by Water" calls up the "drowned Phoenician sailor," ominously designated "your card" by Madame Sosostris, as an object lesson to the protagonist; said to be only "a fortnight dead," Phlebas the Phoenician nevertheless is a stranger to him, and seems to have the weight of a traditional or mythic figure. Finally, in "What the Thunder Said," the protagonist keeps to the present except for one memory, directly confronting his reality of aridity. He has left the familiar scenes with their familiar memories, "plucked" out, walking now not in the city but on a "sandy road," later a "white road," until he arrives at the "empty chapel"; he is indeed on a pilgrimage, seeking rescue from the waste land.

As in Eliot's poem, so in Joyce's novel: after a time something begins to happen. The constant movement of the protagonists ceases to be the repetition of a futile diurnal round, the "walking round in a ring" that the other citizens in both works are presented as continuing to do, and becomes a quest for the way out.

For Stephen the way out would be the freedom of his spirit through the enlightened submission of his will; for Bloom it would be a meaningful life as husband and father through enlightened right action; for Eliot's citizen it would be spiritual transcendence by a means similar (it is significant) to Stephen's. While in the novel the quest involves actual events, in the poem the pilgrimage to the East of Buddha, the Ganges and the Upanishads, to the spiritually fertile sacred land, is apparently a metaphorical one.

The third series of figures common to the two works, of course, is of questers. Both have Odysseus, Siegfried and Dante; *Ulysses* has as well the ghost of King Hamlet, Sinbad the sailor, Daedalus and Icarus, Faust, and one whose presence can be perceived only reflexively from medieval Irish literature or *Finnegans Wake*, the questing avenger Maelduin[65]; *The Waste Land* has the generalized Grail quester, Parsifal, Aeneas, Nerval's "Desdichado," Arnaut, and Kyd's Hieronymo.

The quester is a familiar type in myth and art (the culture of the young has its ski and surf bum, its "easy rider," its itinerant rock singer), and currently it is fashionable to find him everywhere. Furthermore, the allusive method creates fuzzy edges. For example, is one justified in including Maelduin, a literary ghost, in the list of questers in *Ulysses*? Conversely, should one—on the strength of the presence of the wasteland motif, Tiresias and the pattern of references to eyes in the poem—add Oedipus to the list for *The Waste Land*? Finally, the method depends on reinforcement by centrally relevant objects of allusion to make valid the invoking of such figures as Sinbad, Hieronymo, or Arnaut.

But the centrally relevant questers are there, and they predominate. The "song" of the "Thames-daughters" in *The Waste Land* invokes Wagner's *Rheintöchter* and Siegfried, who being spiritually impure fails to return the ring to them and so save the world. Simultaneously it invokes Parsifal, who rejects lustful maidens and secures the Holy Grail. Spiritual blight can be cured only in the spirit, and in both works the spiritual condition of the protagonists is the field on which the crucial issue, What is to become of them? is joined. That is to say, first, that those admirable and successful questers the pilgrim Dante, the good husband and father Odysseus, and the pure hero Parsifal join the true prophets and the saviors as models, guides, and encouragers, respectively, in the proper or enlightened course; and second, that in both works what is centrally important— that proper course for the protagonists' quest—is spiritual or, as we should say, psychological. The third series of figures articulates both a thematic concern common to novel and poem and a common principal field (locus) of action.

Of these the thematic similarity, of a series of questers in each that combines with a series of prophets and saviors to indicate a way the characters may rescue themselves spiritually, is by its nature cosmological, so that the role in *Ulysses* of the two linked series of figures both helps to explain and extends Eliot's statement in *After Strange Gods*, "the most ethically orthodox of the more eminent writers of my time is Mr. Joyce." But this matter is best explored in the context of a formal similarity between the two works other than the allusive "method"; that is the manner in which they both end. That formal similarity, like the formal second similarity embodied in the series of questers, their common psychological locus of action, must wait upon attention to one final manifestation of the allusive "method" in *The Waste Land*: the Notes.

In order to demonstrate the kinship of the Notes with *Ulysses* and with Modernism in general, I shall have to go into some detail; and I am delighted to do so, because a great deal of nonsense has been written about them. Most critics speak of the "notes *to*" *The Waste Land*, indicating their uncertainty about the relationship; Eliot, who was capable of employing language precisely, used the totally ambiguous "on"; my endeavor here is to justify my using the preposition "of" and my capitalizing "Notes" when speaking of them as a totality.

Critical treatment of the Notes of *The Waste Land* has ranged from "for ornithologists even the passage from Chapman would have the advantage of exact description," justifying Eliot's quotation from a description of the hermit-thrush in a standard *Handbook of Birds of Eastern North America* (in the note to line 357)[66] to the succinct advice that "we have license . . . to ignore them."[67] The supposed license derives from Eliot's declared ambivalence about them and "regret" at "having sent so many enquirers off on a wild goose chase after Tarot cards and the Holy Grail." According to the published text, he said in a paper read at the University of Minnesota in 1956:

> I had at first intended only to put down all the references for my quotations, with a view to spiking the guns of critics of my earlier poems who had accused me of plagiarism. Then, when it came to print *The Waste Land* as a little book—for the poem on its first appearance in *The Dial* and in *The Criterion* [which occurred one and two months respectively before the book was published on December 15] had no notes whatever—it was discovered that the poem was inconveniently short, so I set to work to expand the notes, in order to provide a few more pages of printed matter [apparently to fill out a sixty-four-page book, on the suggestion of Roger Fry], with the result that they became the remarkable exposition of bogus scholarship that is still on view today. . . . But I don't think that these notes did any harm to other poets: certainly I cannot think of any good contemporary poet who has abused this same

practice. [As for Miss Marianne Moore, *her* notes to poems are always pertinent, curious, conclusive, delightful and give no encouragement whatever to the researcher of origins.] [Eliot's brackets; apparently an interpolation.] No, it is not because of my bad example to other poets that I am penitent: it is because my notes stimulated the wrong kind of interest among the seekers of sources. It was just, no doubt, that I should pay my tribute to the work of Miss Jessie Weston; but I regret having sent so many enquirers off on a wild goose chase after Tarot cards and the Holy Grail.[68]

I have quoted from the statement at length because in it Eliot himself provided a detailed brief for the dismissing of his own creation to critics who are so minded, one from which they have quoted and requoted phrases toward that end. The Notes originally were mere documentation in the solemn spirit of the notes to *The Shephearde's Calendar* (as distinguished from the ironic spirit of those to *The Dunciad*). The periodical publication of the poem did not include even those. Then he tried to expand them as filler and they became, unfortunately, "bogus scholarship." He "regrets" having inspired "a wild goose chase." Eliot's testimony appears to constitute imposing external evidence that the Notes are best minimized if not indeed ignored.

But are we to take seriously the declaration by a poet (especially a modernist poet) that he created pages of sheer filler? And is his "with the result that they became" a confession that he literally could not avoid "bogus scholarship"? Or does his narrative of an original intention "to provide a few more pages of printed matter" and of a "remarkable exposition of bogus scholarship" that resulted constitute instead a coolly historical account of how a late augmentation of *The Waste Land* actually came about? Is his assertion that no "good contemporary poet" has "abused this same practice" coy modesty, or is it irony? How necessary was his "tribute" to the Weston book, especially in the light of at least one much more pressing claim to "tribute" which he ignored? Finally: the context of this statement about the Notes is a general criticism Eliot was directing at "the seekers of sources" in the study of poetry, and he referred to the Notes as a unique "occasion" on which he was "not guiltless of having led critics into temptation"; so whose fault is the regrettable "wild goose chase" of those avid "seekers" with "the wrong kind of interest"? In other words, is this The Distinguished Poet or Old Possum speaking?

Eliot's statement that he wrote them because "the poem was inconveniently short" engenders speculation about the precise role that Liveright's preference respecting a length for the American edition of *The Waste Land* played in the genesis of the Notes. But it is an injustice to any serious and honest poet for critics to infer from that statement and similar ones by Eliot that an account of their genesis is an abject apology for their existence. Furthermore: not only is it unlikely that Eliot would undertake to provide meretricious filler in order to get out another book; it is also unlikely that even had he been willing, any such filler was required. The Notes occupy only twelve pages in the volume (they begin on page 53); the few pages difference between them and "all the references for my quotations," which he "at first intended . . . to put down," could have been adjusted with the greatest ease by typesetting and a fly leaf or two before the back endpaper (there are now none, and small books of verse do resort to them). Furthermore, the book is composed of sixteen-page gatherings, so that alternatively, barring Liveright's categorical unwillingness, the text proper and the projected "references" could have been printed on forty-eight well-filled pages. Especially in those early days the Woolfs did not weigh commercial considerations heavily; but it is still worth mentioning that the Hogarth Press chose to make the first English edition of *The Waste Land*, published in 1923, only thirty-five pages long.

One possibly unequivocal indication that Eliot did regret and repudiate the Notes remains: their absence from the periodicals. However, there was little reason for his failure to substitute the original "references" if in fact his withholding the full set of Notes (despite his statement, he had developed them before periodical publication) reflects any disquiet on his part. For the editors of the *Dial* were giving him their annual award and so presumably would have been agreeable; and in any case the *Criterion* was his own magazine.

That Eliot's procedure in the periodicals signifies no disquiet about the Notes can be shown beyond reasonable doubt. According to the evidence in Valerie Eliot's introduction to the facsimile edition of the drafts and in other sources, the contract with Liveright to publish *The Waste Land* had been signed well before the arrangement to publish it in the *Dial* was made two months in advance of its appearance there. The *Dial* arrangement resulted from elaborate negotiations, since Liveright had, both contractually and morally, prior rights in a literary property. The arrangement of September 7 was for Liveright to delay book publication slightly and for the *Dial* to publish the poem without the Notes. Furthermore, a letter by Gilbert Seldes, an admirer of the poem who was then managing editor of the *Dial*, establishes not only that the Notes were completed in time for

publication in the magazine but also that they were explicitly denied to
it. On August 31 he wrote to its publisher:

> We must assume that Eliot O.K.'s publication in *The Dial* without the
> notes . . . which are exceedingly interesting and add much to the poem,
> but don't become interested in them because we simply cannot have
> them.[69]

In other words, the Notes were withheld from a prior periodical publication to protect the value of the book, not added later in order to make it
one; and Eliot, an honorable man, could simply have followed suit in
printing the poem in his *Criterion* (which he sent late to its American
subscribers out of consideration for the *Dial*).

Although he did not include the Notes in the manuscript draft material
when he presented it to Quinn, despite the latter's reference in correspondence to "the whole thing, poetry and prose," and more specific "the
MS of The Waste Land and the Notes,"[70] that exclusion is of no significance here. He declared to Quinn that "the manuscript of *The Waste Land*
which I am sending you" was "worth preserving in its present form" because it was "the only evidence of the difference which [Pound's] criticism has made to this poem."[71] The strength of this explicit motive is
measured by the fact that it seems to have grown in importance for him
rather than abated. Thus, although in the same letter he expressed politely
his "hope that the portions which I have suppressed will never appear in
print," according to his widow we owe her edition precisely to this motive:

> We never thought it would turn up, but Tom told me that if it did I was
> to publish it. "It won't do me any good," he added, "but I would like
> people to realise the extent of my debt to Ezra." Originally he had con-
> fided to Quinn that he hoped the portions which he had suppressed
> would never appear in print.[72]

And Pound had nothing to do with the Notes.

To sum up: at the very worst, the available external evidence taken as a
whole does not show conclusively how Eliot himself regarded the Notes,
and so is not even the somewhat qualified guide to how we are to regard
them that conclusive evidence of such a kind would be.

One bit of external evidence very different from Eliot's pronouncement
about the Notes a third of a century later is more useful than an ordinary
statement about his own work, even by this unusually modest and con-

siderate artist, not so much because of the "seriousness" it declares at a time and in circumstances that encourage credence as because of what it reveals inadvertently. To an inquiry from Arnold Bennett about them he replied that "they were serious, and not more of a skit than some things in the poem." Furthermore, apparently feeling when finishing the poem in London that it was too solemn, he intended to introduce it with a doggerel poem by Pound about its composition; but apparently he accepted Pound's dissuasion.[73] In other words, there is evidence that (although with rare exceptions this was not his practice in serious poems) Eliot regarded a "skit" element—literary trifling or play—as admissible to *The Waste Land*. Such a relaxation of the ascetic impulse and attitude behind the poem is gratifying, because its more complex aesthetic and vision are also truer to the artist who, when editing the *Egoist*, wrote and printed pseudonymous silly letters about contributions to generate correspondence, whose light verse before and after *The Waste Land* and fondness for doing imitations and playing pranks are too easily forgotten, and whose widow recalls, "He was always making jokes."[74] Need one be solemn about

> O O O O that Shakespeherian Rag—
> It's so elegant
> So intelligent

in order to appreciate its specific effectiveness as irony and its general effectiveness as a portrayal of cultural debasement?

To Eliot's willingness to admit an element of literary play to *The Waste Land* one must add the fact that despite his demonstrated "theft" of details from *Ulysses* the Notes fail to mention it, and that in addition to *Ulysses* other sources of important lines, details and phrases are not documented. The familiar Psalm 137 begins: "By the rivers of Babylon, there we sat down, yea, we wept"; especially since the draft has only its first phrase, he cannot have been ignorant of the origin of his almost identical line. Or of every single mark of *Ulysses*; anyone unpersuaded by reasonableness need only remind himself of Pound's comments about "J.J." in the drafts. Yet the belief that the Notes are serious documentation (presumably of remarkable stylistic ineptitude) persists stubbornly. "Precisely because some echoes are and others are not acknowledged" one recent critic reaches the opposite conclusion to mine: "the allusions are . . . instinctive or habitual rather than designed."[75] This critic is concerned with the question, discussed earlier, of the nature of the relationship to (influence on) Eliot's work of possible sources in his reading; he provides a cautionary example of the limited scope and limiting effects of "the seek[ing] of sources" for *The Waste Land*. This was Eliot's warning in his University of Minnesota address, which was largely devoted to limitations and fallacies of that concern about *any* poetry.

On the basis of the evidence, it seems reasonable to dismiss the simplistic concept that the Notes are documentation, as well as to conclude that any narrow and solemn view of their possible function may be precisely inadequate. The example of *Ulysses* provides a guide beyond such a view, for the Notes are another element of *The Waste Land* similar to an equivalent element of Joyce's novel, whether or not it influenced Eliot as a model for them.

When Stuart Gilbert accepted solemnly the chart which Joyce fed to him delineating an "organ," "art," "colour," "symbol" and "technic" for each chapter of *Ulysses*; when he reproduced the parts of this chart Joyce permitted in his book *James Joyce's Ulysses*; and when he spent much of his time tracing down random evidence for it, he lacked judgment as well as wit. For such arbitrary patterns, as Edmund Wilson remarked about the chart in his essay on *Ulysses* in *Axel's Castle*, cannot do serious work in a novel. They were not meant to; the chapters are discrete entities in important ways, but that is the result of the serious work which is being done in each chapter by a particular set of allusions or a particular narrative method. And treating with solemn critical respect the bare assertion of Joyce's chart that the "organ" of the chapter in which Bloom sautés a kidney is "Kidney," and of the chapter in which the Citizen throws a biscuit tin, "Muscle," is precisely analogous to saying that Eliot's quotation from Chapman's *Handbook of Birds* would gratify ornithologists.

Yet to some extent the arbitrary patterns exist, claiming asylum and sanction from those qualities of their respective chapters that do establish integrity. The question of what Joyce actually was trying to encompass in his sequence of chapters is—as is usual with *Ulysses*—complicated. Yet, the question must be confronted in order to elucidate that element in the novel similar to Eliot's Notes. Richard Ellmann has addressed himself to this question in his recent book *Ulysses on the Liffey* (New York: Oxford, 1972). He also has published the different chart which Joyce sent to his Italian translator and friend Carlo Linati in September 1920. This chart was compiled before the familiar chart loaned to Larbaud (who was preparing his effort on the book's behalf) as *Ulysses* neared publication a year later, then circulated privately in copies for a decade, and finally enshrined in Gilbert's book. The Linati chart has more detail than the Larbaud-Gilbert one, and is less deceptive about what Joyce actually did in the novel. For example, whereas for the third chapter the Larbaud chart shows Menelaus as the Homeric analogue to the Irish nationalist mentioned there, Kevin Egan, in the Linati chart *"Menelao"* appears alone, and so his true and extremely functional correspondence to Stephen at least is not obscured.[76]

However, the Linati chart cannot answer the question about what the arbitrary patterns may be for. It is only less facetious than its more familiar successor. For example, the three chapters devoted to Stephen that begin *Ulysses* are roughly simultaneous with the next three, devoted to Bloom; yet Joyce designates the two groups respectively *"Alba"* and *"Mattina."* Professor Ellmann navigates more by independent sightings than by reliance on this "schema" (or the other), and he is sophisticated and erudite, so that his discussion of Bloom and the kidney (p. 32), for example, is persuasive where Gilbert's smacks of inept special pleading. Professor Ellmann postulates an ingenious pattern of accretions, "parallelism" and "contraries" in the sequence of chapters which makes the novel an intricate systematic embodiment of general concepts, philosophical propositions, and more.

Joyce had a picture of the city of Cork framed in cork. He was being not just witty but metaphysical, in the sense of the term that is both philosophical and literary; and a writer with such a view of the relationship between language and reality (it was probably a major reason for his increasing commitment to the allusive method in successive works) may well have endeavored to achieve a kind of encyclopedism in his novel. That endeavor *would* explain what it is Joyce wished to encompass in his sequence of chapters when he provided for each an arbitrary "organ," "art," "colour" and so forth in addition to their functional patterns.

Pound drew a strong connection with Flaubert's unfinished "Encyclopedia in the form of farce," *Bouvard et Pécuchet,* in the title and text of his French essay on *Ulysses,* "James Joyce et Pécuchet." But as the description of the novel in *Ulysses on the Liffey* suggests, likening *Ulysses* to the encyclopedic statire of *Bouvard et Pécuchet* raises a problem that Pound fails to acknowledge. For Joyce does seem to some extent, despite the mischievousness of his charts, his comicality and playfulness on virtually every page, and his widely ranging mockery of modern civilization in the manner of Flaubert, in dead earnest. To some still uncertain extent he did seriously (with dubious success at best, I think) attempt to achieve, by incremental patterns through the successive chapters, an encyclopedic inclusiveness in his novel. He declares it, in fact. When he specifies that the good father Purefoy is the model of right action for Bloom, he does so as a ventriloquist; for a major reason why there is a sequence of parodies of English prose styles in the fourteenth chapter is to provide masks through which the author can make statements about the revellers in the maternity hospital, especially the two with whom he is most concerned. (He condemns contraception and adultery as Eliot does, but celebrates erotic love and procreation.) In that specification the dummy of Carlyle not only addresses Purefoy directly but also, appropriately, makes reference to the novel itself:

> By heaven, Theodore Purefoy, thou hast done a doughty deed and no botch! Thou art, I vow, the remarkablest progenitor barring none in this chaffering allincluding most farraginous chronicle.[77]

The last phrase is frequently quoted. It describes Joyce's chronicle of Bloom's and Stephen's day as, to take the multisyllabled epithets in reverse order: formed of various materials (the "method"), encyclopedic, and a bandying of (playing with) words. There is no reason why he should be serious in the manifestly accurate first and third designations and not so in the second one. The informative phrase itself (like the ventriloquist's parodic strategy) also is playful, of course; simultaneously. And this fact reminds one that while the arbitrary patterns in his allincluding chronicle are Joyce's own, the solemnity about them was contributed by others.

The precise combination remains open to question, but Joyce's encyclopedism combines playfulness with a serious intent. That fact distinguishes *Ulysses* strikingly from Flaubert's satiric "Encyclopedia in the form of farce," and has a broader significance as well. In addition to comparing *Ulysses* to *Bouvard et Pécuchet*, "James Joyce et Pécuchet" mentions three novels filled with literary play: *Gargantua, Don Quixote* and *Tristram Shandy*. Justly, for like Joyce in *Ulysses*, Rabelais, Cervantes and Sterne were playful in those novels not because they were frivolous artists but because they were serious artists—that is, were serious as artists; they loved language and appreciated the formal possibilities of fictional narrative. The catalogues in *Gargantua*, the parodies and burlesques (already mentioned) in *Don Quixote*, and the typographical tricks and play with conventions of the novel in *Tristram Shandy* are all in *Ulysses*.

Nevertheless the striking difference between the playful yet very serious encyclopedism of *Ulysses* and Flaubert's satiric "farce" illuminates a more important difference from Cervantes and Sterne, if not from Rabelais. Their play was created for its own sake as a quality of their art; Joyce's modernist play had to be work as well. That is to say, his parodies, burlesques, tricks, and manipulations of the conventions of the novel as a genre are not only play that points outward to a particular writer, literary form or real situation; they are also and *primarily*—like his patterns of allusion—purposeful work that functions within *Ulysses*. Only his occasional Rabelaisian catalogues seem to exist for the sheer delight in them (of writer as well as reader, one guesses).

Perhaps even the playfulness is functional, as winning acceptance for the parodies and the rest; certainly, critics admired most of those various virtuosities in the novel for themselves alone long before the ways in which they work were understood. In any case, the element of working play is everywhere in the novel. And in the Notes of *The Waste Land* it is the means Eliot eventually adopted to relieve the solemnity of his poem and simultaneously to employ the "method" for focus, reinforcement, enrichment. The fact is that what he asserts about Marianne Moore's notes to her poems in his apparently denigrating account of his own Notes actually (playfully) describes the Notes of *The Waste Land*: "pertinent, curious, conclusive, delightful and giv[ing] no encouragement whatever to the researcher of origins."

It is Eliot's modernist assumption—expressed in the very term "method"—that allusions ought to be given important work, his concern to use a source not celebrate it, which explains the absence of reference to *Ulysses* and Psalm 137 in the Notes: his poem had nothing to gain from citing the former; the nationalism and violence of the latter would positively work against the poem. And it is the element of play which makes some notes pedantically precise:

> The currants were quoted at a price " carriage and insurance free to London"; and the Bill of Lading, etc., were to be handed to the buyer upon payment of the sight draft

some notes casually vague:

> The following lines were stimulated by the account of one of the Antarctic expeditions (I forget which, but I think one of Shackleton's) . . . .

some notes pompous:

> The interior of St. Magnus Martyr is to my mind one of the finest among Wren's interiors . . . .

and some chatty:

> A phenomenon which I have often noticed.

It is the element of play, also, that causes Eliot sometimes to use "V." and "Cf." indiscriminately, that has a note to line 126 refer the reader back, apparently pointlessly, to lines 37 and 48, and that cites "To His Coy Mistress" the second time it is invoked (line 196) but not the first time (line 185).

These are not errors, for in both the (independent) 1963 editions of the *Collected Poems* such errors as the failure to count a line and the mistaken line reference in a note have been corrected. As in the case of play in *Ulysses*, all this playful inconsistency in the Notes is primarily functional. Thus, in some instances Eliot really wants the reader to "see" (bring to mind) and in others to "compare" (think of the details of) the work cited. Where his purpose is instead to associate specific material with the poem, he cites the source *in order to quote* what he wishes from it, whimsically using either "V." or "Cf." on those occasions since the material is there in the note itself. And where a cited source is not made to do direct work for the poem, the citation of the classic title adds it to the fabric of allusions to artifacts of civilization. Similarly, the line *before* 126 ("Those are pearls that were his eyes") is identical with line 48 except that it lacks a final word, which therefore gains attention ("Look!"); and given that hint one goes to two lines after 37 (to read "and my eyes failed"), and so discovers the pattern of eye and blindness imagery that runs through the poem. Finally, the playful annotation of "To His Coy Mistress" at the second allusion is primarily functional; for the note to line 197, the line immediately following that second instance, quotes from the work of a minor contemporary of Donne's a passage that invokes Actaeon and Diana, so that the scope of the allusion to Marvell's seduction poem is controlled, limited to what will enrich *The Waste Land*.

Working backwards through the four notes quoted above: "A phenomenon which I have often noticed" is a subtle statement of the speaker's frequent awareness of the sacrifice of Jesus (much like the appearance to

Stephen of the three-masted schooner with "crosstrees" at the end of the
third chapter of *Ulysses*), for Jesus died at the ninth hour, according to the
Gospels, and the note is to "Saint Mary Woolnoth kept the hours/With a
dead sound on the final stroke of nine." The pompous comment on the
interior of St. Magnus Martyr is followed by citation of a book (actually,
it was a London County Council pamphlet[78]) entitled significantly *The
Proposed Demolition of Nineteen City Churches*. The vague reference to
an Antarctic expedition introduces a passage (the "lines were stimulated" probably by an account at the end of Chapter 10 of Shackleton's
South) declaring that the members of the expedition had, when "at the
extremity of their strength," the "constant delusion" that someone else
was with them. Finally, the pedantic talk about currants "carriage and in-
surance free to London" reinforces the parent passage in "The Fire Sermon" about the homosexual "Smyrna merchant" with currants "C.i.f.
London," to prepare for the contrasting "Death by Water" far in time and
place from London of another Levantine trader, "Phlebas the Phoenician,"
who:

> Forgot the cry of gulls . . .
> And the profit and loss.
>   A current under sea

There is no opportunity or reason to demonstrate here the functional
nature of every single note, even if it is in my power to do so. Eliot's strategies vary. The first two notes refer the reader to major prophetic books
of the Old Testament, and in those two cases the passage of external
material merely cited in the Notes is important, as I shall try to show. Beyond these initial modest demands, "the researcher of origins" has little of
any importance to occupy him. Certain notes contain irrelevant material, a
playful device which enables the poet to slip in statements that do real
work in his poem; for example, the ornithological note about the hermit-
thrush mentioned earlier ends: "Its 'water-dripping song' is justly celebrated." Other notes just as artfully employ a playful stylistic ineptitude
reminiscent of certain chapters of *Ulysses* (especially the two before the
last) to hide such truly operant statements in punning and innuendo, as do
the first and fourth of the examples just discussed. Some notes simply add
to the fabric of cultural allusions. Some invoke particular sources because
of the allusive enrichment to be derived from a general association of the
work named with the poem: for example, *The Tempest*. Some, such as

those quoting the obscure John Day on Actaeon and Diana and the eminent J. A. Froude on Elizabeth and Essex, and the early ones with quotations from Baudelaire and the *Inferno* that elaborate the vision of the City, work for expansion and enrichment of meaning by bringing specific passages of external material into direct relation with the poem. Some, like the headnote and the discussions of the Tarot pack and Tiresias, seem to be clumsy exposition; but these are more valuable for what they suggest (a quest, prophecy, enlightenment, respectively) than for what they say respectively about "the Grail legend," "the Fisher King himself" or the narrative strategy of the poem. Some references are made at least partly for the reinforcement offered by the cited title itself, such as those to *The White Devil, Götterdämmerung, Les Fleurs du Mal* and *Paradise Lost.* Some notes work to enrich the poem by using a phrase in it as a pretext (such as that to "the walls/Of Magnus Martyr"). And some have the function of pointing out connections and creating emphasis and focus—typically for the Notes, by indirect and often playful means.

My purpose in this long discussion of the Notes has been to suggest their nature and their function, that they are brilliantly "of" *The Waste Land*. But it is no digression: to indicate their nature and function is to return to the relationship between Eliot's poem and *Ulysses*. For the Notes are principally another use of the allusive method; in them the poem has, like *Ulysses*, an element of play; and as in *Ulysses* the play is subordinate to, if not actually an agent of, serious artistic work. Perhaps at this point —with the demonstration that the novel and the poem have in common (1) a "method" crucial to both, (2) certain kinds of theme and action, and (3) certain attitudes toward the range of material and artistic strategies possible for a work of literature—some of the lineaments of the joint cultural role of *Ulysses* and *The Waste Land* can be discerned.

6

WORLD WITHOUT END

*If it is not a novel, that is . . . because the novel,
instead of being a form, was simply the expression
of an age which had not sufficiently lost all form
to feel the need of something stricter.*

The first of Eliot's Notes is to the beginning of God's discourse to Ezekiel as the "Son of man"; the second is to a passage in the twelfth and final chapter of the Book of the unknown prophet, *Ecclesiastes*, which describes a waste land (12:5). Before ending a few verses later, the chapter reads:

> And moreover, because the preacher was wise, he still taught the people knowledge . . . and set in order many proverbs.
> The preacher sought to find out acceptable words . . . .
> The words of the wise are as goads . . . which are given from one shepherd. (12:9-11)

The allusive enrichment provided by these three verses increases in the next two, which are almost the last words of the prophet. The twelfth verse is an ironic commentary on the Notes themselves, Eliot's "bogus scholarship." The thirteenth combines with and redirects the twelfth to pronounce judgment on that of which the Notes as play are a parody—the secular learning of modern civilized man, out of which he has made his waste land—and to instruct the citizen respecting his civilization and the right course for him, in terms consonant with what we know about the poem:

> And further, by these, my son, be admonished: of making many books there is no end; and much study is a weariness of the flesh.
> Let us hear the conclusion of the whole matter: Fear God, and keep his commandments: for this is the whole duty of man. (12:12-13)

The religious nature of *The Waste Land* is readily accepted, for we know Eliot's later poetry and we know of his conversion and religious activities. In contrast, Joyce had been through orthodoxy and would have none of it (he extracted a promise from his wife that she would not permit even the mere presence of a priest at his burial). Yet it has been pointed out that *Ulysses* has precisely the sets of prophets, saviors, and questers, the basic situation for the protagonists, and the general pattern of action that *The Waste Land* has. And I can no longer postpone my assertion that, though it is not an orthodox novel in any doctrinal sense, *Ulysses* is religious. I mean that the rescue of Leopold Bloom and Stephen Dedalus from a state of helplessness in the predicament that is destroying each of those men of the modern City is a story of salvation.

At the very end of the third chapter, for example, Stephen turns and sees the three "crosstrees" when he has a sense that he is being watched; and in that chapter he is made analogous to Menelaus, who wrestled with Proteus for a prophecy. Proteus's prophecy (in the language of the Butcher and Lang translation popular in the first part of the century) was:

> Nay, surely thou shouldst have done goodly sacrifice to Zeus . . . . For it is not thy fate to see thy friends . . . till thou hast . . . offered holy hecatombs to the deathless gods who keep the wide heaven.[79]

That is what Stephen comes to do by the end of the novel. Just before he sees the "crosstrees" of the three-masted schooner, he remembers a dream he had the night before; when Bloom first crosses his path, at the point in the novel at which the two characters start to break out of their futile diurnal round, he remembers it as a dream of deliverance: "Last night I flew. Easily flew." Ultimately the dream is fulfilled, at an unexpected time and in an unexpected way. And Stephen is freed to "offer holy hecatombs."

Stephen's problem had never been that which *Ecclesiastes* called "the whole duty of man," for he was terrified of God. But Catholic catechisms say in answer to the question (variously put) about man's basic purpose in life that it is, always in the same order, to know God, love God, and serve God. In the *Portrait* Stephen had said "I will not serve"; and a little later, continuing to reverse the order in the catechisms, "—I tried to love God, he said at length. It seems now I failed." In *Ulysses*, the fulfillment of his dream, an action presented as (I say with conviction but trepidation) miracle, enables him finally to begin at the proper first stage in the sequence.[80]

I can do no more here than barely sketch some elements of an action that leads to the possibility of salvation in the case of Stephen, and cannot do even as much in the more complicated case of Bloom. However, he too is ultimately, in the phrase of *Ecclesiastes* that is the Old Testament equivalent of "serve God," and which Joyce makes especially appropriate to him, able to "keep [God's] commandments."

Eliot said in one of his Norton lectures at Harvard in 1933 that Joyce was "concerned with the relation of man to God."[81] In the process of discussing similarities between *Ulysses* and his poem, I have, possibly, made Eliot's assertion seem a tenable one and shown another similarity. Lionel Trilling has written, "more than with anything else, our literature is concerned with salvation."[82]

The point must be made and emphasized that Joyce does not, nor does Eliot in *The Waste Land*, adopt Christian doctrine or even assume the Christian cosmology. Both are only hypostatizing the salvation of the questing protagonists, which requires help from beyond the world. And in both works the outcome of the characters' quest is suggested but not presented. Stephen is freed to make his way; Bloom is made able and eager to change his relationship with Molly, who ultimately is moved to give him the chance. In each case Joyce has literally presented a miracle (at any rate, a specific unexplainable coincidence that is salvational) to rescue the character from helpless, slow destruction, and has left him with a new opportunity. The last lines of *The Waste Land*, like the corresponding parts of the stories of Bloom and Stephen, are subtle and complex, but seem to embody much the same combination of likelihood without finality.

Before considering the implications of the similarity in the ways the two works end, it will be constructive to examine some evidence that what *The Waste Land* finally presents is potential salvation, for that proposition is by no means a critical consensus.

In the first place, the protagonist's gradual relinquishing of memories of the past in favor of acting in the present is consonant with a redemptive resolution. The titles of the five sections also seem to bear out the pattern of helpless predicament followed by change. In the first section the dead are burying their dead; in the second life is static, a set of procedures without meaning or real value. Then in the third something happens, a fiery sermon supplants the games of chess, bringing a painful heightened awareness of things ("O Lord thou pluckest/burning") very much like those experienced by Bloom in Davy Byrne's pub and Stephen in the National Library (eighth and ninth chapters of *Ulysses*). In the fourth Phlebas is invoked, dead by water, not buried under ground, and is said to have "entered" a spiral pattern like the purgatorial stair in Dante (and in "Ash Wednesday"). The title of the fifth and last section refers to a change in the world outside the quester and a message from above.

Taken by itself this account proves nothing and is at least slightly tendentious; but the last section of the poem, which Eliot composed with such clear purpose and control, has considerable evidence of good fortune. It begins with a verse paragraph suggesting the arrest of Jesus in Gethsemane, the crucifixion, and the quester's consequent despair. There follows a long paragraph about the wasted nature of the land and "dry sterile thunder" from the sky, expressing the quester's wish for water, and ending "But there is no water." But the third paragraph presents a suggestion of Jesus's apparition to the disciples on the road to Emmaus, reinforced by the note about an Antarctic expedition—an evocation of the resurrected Christ's power and mercy. Then, following an apocalyptic paragraph about the destruction of our spiritually "unreal" civilization, and another presenting what seems to be a remembered nightmare that ends with "exhausted wells," the implications for the quester are correspondingly negative: he ends his pilgrimage at "the empty chapel," apparently unsuccessful. It is the home of "only the wind"; "only a cock" is there.

The conjunction is significant. The wind, "un*heard*" in "the brown land" (1.175), is a Christian (and Judaic) emblem of the breath of God or Holy Spirit, and Eliot uses it so (the breath that speaks the Word) in "Ash Wednesday." The cock is a medieval Christian emblem (with Greek and Roman ancestry) of the annunciation both of enlightenment and of God's saving advent. According to Saint Ambrose, with the crowing of the cock, "hope returns to all" and "Jesus regards the hesitant and corrects the wanderers."[83] Finally, in those (less corrupted) versions of the Grail legend which include the perilous chapel, the quester arrives in a storm; storms normally include rain, lightning, then the thunder of that lightning; and they begin with wind.

Promptly the presumption of the quester's repeated "only" is made plain. For the cock crows an annunciation, which the poem links grammatically to light from the cosmos; and the cock's fellow, the wind, is seen to have been announcing the imminence of both that light, whose sound will follow, and rain—pure water, falling on the waste land, coming from above. The passage reads:

> Only a cock stood on the rooftree
> Co co rico co co rico
> In a flash of lightning. Then a damp gust
> Bringing rain.

Whether the momentary gust does or does not bring all the rain that falls is not indicated. This contributes to the effect of likelihood without finality that, as was stated above, is created by an inconclusive ending to the poem: the quester may have heard the subsequent thunder not merely after but through rain, falling continuously from heaven, with all that that signifies traditionally and in *The Waste Land*.

The indefiniteness is achieved in part through a change in the poem, a change that also stresses the importance of the depicted annunciation and advent of rain: with the mention of the cock, the poem undergoes a transition forward in time. The quester suddenly begins speaking in the past tense, declaring that the cock "stood"; and, of the remaining specific occurrences before it ends, that the storm thunder "spoke" and then that he "sat fishing." The changing relationship that the poem reveals before the quester's arrival at the chapel, between his memories of figures and events in the past and his confrontation with his reality, has been discussed above. In this final section nothing but the remembered nightmare has interrupted his presentation of his experience as it is unfolding. Now suddenly the present time of *The Waste Land* becomes past time: what has been unfolding, the pilgrim's quest for salvation, itself becomes something remembered. The speaker recounts what happened to him once when he arrived at an "empty chapel": there was wind, a cock crowed, and so forth. The effect is to suggest the powerful significance for him of that experience. It brought his quest to a conclusion; and it made possible the future condition in the final present time of the poem, out of which he can reflect back on that conclusion.

Two paragraphs remain to the poem. The first of them presents the protagonist's memory of and reflections on what the thunder said on that significant occasion. The final paragraph recalls his subsequent fishing and presents fragments he asserts "I have shored against my ruins."

The three words from the *Upanishad* once heard through the thunder, and rendered "Give, sympathise, control" in the Notes, are treated in the paragraph devoted to them as though they concern respectively the capacities for commitment, for love, and for submission "To controlling hands." The *Upanishad* in question has this last as the first in the sequence, and it actually means "self-control"[84] ; Eliot's alterations are significant both of his concern with obedience to "Another" (Dante's *"altrui,"* which Eliot rendered so and used in his essay "Dante" and in the published drafts[85]) and also of his desire to present the submission to control as a consequence of the two accompanying spiritual achievements: after commitment and then love, "your heart would have responded / Gaily." As a result of his alterations the passage becomes strikingly like the sequence of "know God, love God, serve God" in the catechism, which is so relevant to Stephen's situation in *Ulysses*.

His spiritual instruction completed, the quester sat, as he says at the beginning of the last paragraph, fishing, the arid plain, he also says, being then behind him; and the poem ends in the series of lines and half-lines. These lines, though brief, are packed with meaning. For example, "O swallow swallow" makes not only a reference to escape, by way of Tennyson's "O swallow, swallow, could I but follow" and of the escape of Philomela (or, in some versions, Procne) through metamorphosis into a swallow, but also a punning suggestion of the actual way of escape: Communion. The line from the *Purgatorio* about a refining fire is preceded there by Arnaut's talk about his remorse for the past, suffering in the present, and hope for the future. The swallow line follows, expressing the hope for escape and for metamorphosis. The line from Gérard de Nerval and the next two deal with the nature of *The Waste Land* itself: the "Desdichado" likens himself to different bereft people in Nerval's poem; *The Waste Land* has been composed of "fragments"—extracts, and disjointed lines and passages; and Hieronymo's "Ile fit you" is his response to a request for a play (in *The Spanish Tragedy*), which he then suggests be presented with the actors all speaking different languages. But the three lines also function in the story of the quester: the speaker of Nerval's poem remembers a consoler, and contact with the supernatural; the fragments are said to be a bulwark against "ruins"; Hieronymo's son, the victim of a treacherous hanging in a garden, is analogous to Jesus and the savior gods; and the avenging father says of his play to be spoken in many languages, in response to the complaint that it is "mere confusion": "the conclusion/Shall prove the invention and all was good."[86]

Following this, only two lines remain to the poem: the character himself pronounces the three words of spiritual instruction that have been given him by the thunder—plain evidence of a beginning; and, finally, the word rendered in the Notes as "The Peace which passeth understanding" is repeated three times, in the fashion of the conclusion of an *Upanishad* or sacred text of spiritual guidance.

Eliot described the last section of *The Waste Land* as "not the best part, but the only part that justifies the whole, at all."[87] To attempt to present a fully satisfactory account of the whole poem casually here would be presumptuous, and insulting to others who have argued with courteous expatiation. But it is in the last section that any resolution of the earlier developments in the poem must occur. And my hope is that the relatively less sketchy treatment of that section, and a few new critical observations, have succeeded in indicating that something does seem to happen to the protagonist.

If so, then my relevant purpose has been served, which is to make the point that, as in *Ulysses*, nothing definite has happened when the poem ends—that once again an opportunity has been provided, rescue from helpless destruction granted, but the hero's destiny not definitely resolved, his story not concluded.

Eliot had ended such earlier poems as "Prufrock" and "Portrait of a Lady" in a less overt but similar way, and the unresolved end of Joyce's *Portrait* was achieved through subtle undercutting of Stephen's final boast in the immediately preceding pages. The suspended (or inconclusive) ending was as characteristic a quality of modernist literature as has become the extension of it, the "open" ending—indeed "open" form in general—in the poetry and fiction of our own time. The poems by Yeats that are unresolved debates or that end with a question, Paul Morel's suddenly heading toward the city at the end of *Sons and Lovers*, the waiting of the people of *Heartbreak House* for the bombers to return at the final curtain: these are examples in poetry, fiction and drama that come immediately to mind. What one critic calls "the non-assertive conclusion" as a characteristic of literature since the beginning of the century has now begun to receive attention.[88] And it is yet another similarity between *Ulysses* and *The Waste Land*. The description by the same critic of "hidden closure," where the poet will avoid the expressive qualities of strong closure while securing, in various ways, the reader's sense of the poem's integrity.[89]

is a nice account of the case in both works: they end, but the substantial concerns with which they deal are given no final disposition. The passage from Eliot's own essay quoted at the head of this section suggests that a modernist writer's confrontation with reality might make an inconclusive resolution to his portrayal of that reality seem often the only strictly appropriate one. Indeed "something stricter," the inconclusive ending is the "expression" of what was a new "age."

7

PRESENCES

. . . in creation you are responsible for what you can do with material which you must simply accept. And in this material I include the emotions and feelings of the writer himself. . . .

The point has been made, and other things said have borne it out, that the essential locus of action in both *Ulysses* and *The Waste Land* is psychological: what happens in both works is that each protagonist recognizes then admits to himself certain truths about the cosmos and himself, and finally makes a certain resolution for the future. Another similarity between the two works is corollary to this: in both *Ulysses* and *The Waste Land* the essential vehicle of the psychological action is the consciousness of the protagonists. More than of anything else in the poem, the ultimately suppressed epigraph from "Heart of Darkness" would have been "somewhat elucidative" (as Eliot called the passage in the exchange of letters with Pound) of this pair of facts about it.[90]

The direct representation of a character's consciousness follows ultimately from a prominent practice among modernist writers: concealment of the authorial voice through manipulation of the narrative point of view to create the illusion of an autonomous work. Both the title of Hugh Kenner's book on Eliot, *The Invisible Poet*, and Stephen Dedalus's depiction of the artist "within or behind" his work, "invisible, refined out of existence . . . paring his fingernails" are relevant here.

The allusive "method" is manifestly fundamental to *Ulysses* and *The Waste Land*. But as shaper of the formal characteristics of each it is scarcely more so than their authors' manipulation of point of view, which derives from both the endeavor of portraying consciousness itself and the general modernist practice of concealing the authorial voice. In *Ulysses* that dual purpose shapes not only Bloom's and Stephen's monologues and fantasies, which with their carefully built associative and allusive patterns dart from subject to subject while they simultaneously disrupt all action and exposition, but also the novel's variation of narrative styles. Similarly, the sudden shifts and juxtapositions within and between lines in *The Waste Land* are as attributable to the manipulation of point of view as to the "method"; even the stylistically discontinuous Notes are so because they lack an identifiable single authorial voice.

These examples of the effect on novel and poem of the manipulation of point of view suggest a relationship between it and the "method." And they suggest more strongly the presence of an almost unavoidable stylistic complement to it that is also concomitant with the creation of a montage of allusive bits and pieces, a third fundamental determinant of the formal characteristics of each work, the determinant largely responsible for the first quality in either to strike the reader: its texture.

Narrative, logical and rhetorical discontinuity, the disruption of linear progression, is so apparent in *Ulysses* and *The Waste Land* and so prominent a trait of modernist literature as to require no more than mention in the service of comprehensiveness, were it simply a deliberate effect, present in them for its own sake. Perhaps neither Joyce nor Eliot would have abstained from creating discontinuity for its own sake, to judge from certain earlier works of each. And the arch-modernist Pound's assiduous cultivation of it in the prosody of *The Waste Land* has been mentioned.

However, this discontinuity is not independently present. It is symbiotic with both the "method" and the manipulation of point of view, and is largely generated by the latter. Furthermore, in it they meet and accommodate each other. The significant truth about *Ulysses*, *The Waste Land* and Modernism includes that intricate relationship among the three principal determinants of the modernist formal characteristics of each work, especially the unavoidable complementary role that the disruption of linear progression plays in the manipulation of point of view.

One criticism that can be raised against Joyce as manipulator of point of view is that he may draw attention to himself precisely because of the ingenuity of his system of masks behind masks. But *The Waste Land* presents more fundamental problems, for they concern its very coherence. The texture of narrative discontinuity is complicated by an apparent multiplicity of narrators and dramatic speakers who are not clearly identified; and the complication is compounded by inconsistent designation of their speeches. The resolution of those problems lies in the answer to a question avoided before this point by my use of "quester" and "protagonist" to refer to a person or persons unknown: Who is (or are)—to frame the unasked question—the ultimate speaker(s) of what is spoken in *The Waste Land*, its controlling consciousness(es) and voice(s)? *The Waste Land* cannot be discussed with true authority unless this question is answered.

The "different voices" which Eliot stressed when he adopted Dickens's "He do the Police in Different Voices" as a temporary title have caused some to conceive the protagonist-speaker as a composite representative citizen, "Everyman" (as Bloom was so crudely called for so long) both female and male. According to this conception, Marie of the opening paragraph and the "Son of man" addressed in the next paragraph can both be that Everyperson; either of them can be the companion of the neurasthenic woman in "A Game of Chess," and they can be joined in their role as composite speaker by the lower-class woman who holds forth in that same section.

But even if this is the case, who addresses the "Son of man" at the beginning of the second paragraph? When the hyacinth girl speaks it is within quotation marks and directed to the ultimate speaker, indicating that she is not part of him/her but someone remembered. Yet, why is what Madame Sosostris said to the speaker not in quotation marks although it is being related by him/her and he/she uses quotation marks when quoting him/herself? Finally, how is one to integrate Tiresias, who, according to Eliot's note, "not indeed a 'character,' is yet the most important personage in the poem, uniting all the rest"? The poem is said to be about many individuals; and Tiresias is said to be both distinct from all of them and a "personage" who unites all of them. Later in the note it is asserted that "What Tiresias *sees*, in fact, is the substance of the poem." Taken simply, this note confounds the apparent confusion; and partly on the strength of it, some believe that Tiresias is the ultimate speaker.[91]

The Notes, of course, are not to be taken simply. Nevertheless, there is evidence that even before its dramatic metamorphosis Eliot had trouble controlling his complicated strategy in the poem. On the carbon copy of the "Fire Sermon" draft, Pound took him to task for the line "Across her brain one half-formed thought may pass" (which became line 251, "Her brain allows one half-formed thought to pass"), cancelling and circling "may." and commenting in the margin, "make up / yr. mind." then beneath a drawn line, "you Tiresias / if you know / know damn well / or / else you / don't" (p. 46).

I am unable to explain the inconsistent use of quotation marks, but I believe that Eliot's complex modernist strategy of point of view in *The Waste Land* can be shown to be essentially coherent. The point of view he created is one of only three possible alternatives. Either the ultimate speaker of the poem 1) is a single anonymous peripatetic witness-protagonist, as I have represented him; or 2) he/she is a composite of the characters in the poem, as some believe, or 3) he is Tiresias, as others maintain. Before discussing the first two of these, I shall try to demonstrate that the last is not, strictly speaking, a distinct alternative.

That Tiresias is indeed central, as the note about him claims, is declared wittily by the poet. *The Waste Land* has four hundred thirty-four lines (there are ten lines between numbers 350 and 360 in early texts), so that lines 217 and 218 are its middle. And at the very midpoint, the beginning of line 218, one reads, "I Tiresias"; the note is to that line, of course. What is still to be determined is: In what sense is Tiresias not a "character" and yet the uniter and "most important personage" who "sees" the "substance" of the poem?

Being blind, Tiresias can only "see" (the word is italicized in the note) in the sense of the seer; and indeed it is only that sort of sight that will be of value in the waste land. The first appearance of "a mere spectator" in the poem (as the note calls Tiresias is at the beginning of its second paragraph, where the speaker is addressed as "Son of man." That phrase has the first line-note, "Cf. Ezekiel 2:1." And there is no better evidence that the Notes are working play than Eliot's having caused to follow the expansive and oblique headnote, a note that contrasts with that one only by its irreducible terseness, but also by its directness and its eloquent significance.

Identified by the phrase "Son of man" and the note, Ezekiel is associated with Tiresias—anticipates him in fact—as the prophet who addresses the speaker. But that phrase is used about eighty times in *Ezekiel,* as well as elsewhere in the Old Testament (often to refer to the Messiah), and Jesus uses it as many times in the Gospels to refer to himself. My point is that the one particular passage cited in the note is itself the reason for the citation:

And he said unto me, Son of man, stand upon thy feet, and I will speak unto thee.

And the spirit entered into me when he spake unto me, and set me upon my feet, that I heard him that spake unto me. (2:1-2)

The passage is richly significant. God tells Ezekiel, the "Son of man," to stand and hear Him, but in doing so grants His grace to make it possible, a sequence which is reminiscent of the annunciation and spiritually guiding thunder at the end of the poem. Even more germane here: the passage can be taken to mean not that Ezekiel heard God's words from on high as a result of the spirit's having entered him, but that the spirit of God itself which entered him is the "him that" Ezekiel heard, speaking God's words within him—that the speaking in question is a state of consciousness; and Ezekiel the prophet, whose sacred Book begins "Now it came to pass . . . as I was among the captives by the river of Chebar" (1:1), is also the "Son of man." The association of the phrase with the Old Testament Messiah and with Jesus serves to reinforce its salutary significance: the Messiah saves; Jesus is both a prophet and the Christ or Messiah; and God dwells (permanently) in Jesus.

My point is perhaps clear: if the prophet in the note to line 20 is himself the "Son of man," then the "Son of man" in line 20 himself is the prophet. The "spectator" who addresses the "Son of man," who warns through the voice of the bartender "HURRY UP PLEASE ITS TIME," and who points to Phlebas as an object lesson, he who has "perceived," "foretold" and "foresuffered all," is inside the subject of the poem, whether that subject and ultimate speaker is single or multiple, talks to him from within his mind. Furthermore, the prophet within him is the spirit of God within him, because, as the passage from *Ezekiel* stresses, it is the spirit of God that is the prophetic power, or as *Ecclesiastes* puts it, "The words of the wise . . . are given from one shepherd." Tiresias indeed "unites all the rest" and is "the most important personage in the poem"; taken in this light, the note is as playful as any.

Joyce developed his portrayal of his subject's consciousness and his manipulation of point of view when he went from *Portrait* to *Ulysses*. Similarly, Eliot's dramatic representation of the voice within his subject's consciousness had been achieved in a simpler form (and a secular context) in "Prufrock," in which the voice seems to be that of Prufrock's fears and inhibitions. In *The Waste Land*, where the voice is associated with the prophet of *Ecclesiastes*, Ezekiel, the Old Testament Messiah and Jesus, and identified as Tiresias, who prophesied to Odysseus and tried to guide and save Oedipus, the context is spiritual. The voice transmits the three words in the thunder; and when those words are adopted as the last utterance in the poem of the questing subject, it pronounces a concluding benediction. The voice is that of one's personal prophet or "good angel," the voice of virtue, which is to say of conscience and wisdom, the Christian Holy Spirit and Hebrew *Shechinah*, the indwelling divine Presence. The epigraph from Petronius that Eliot finally selected for *The Waste Land* is apt not only because the sibyl's terrible circumstances correspond to the spiritual condition of the denizens of his waste land, but also because she is both a human being in despair and a prophet; and so the epigraph announces the relationship of protagonist and prophet in the poem that follows.

Reflection on the view that Tiresias is the ultimate speaker and controlling consciousness of *The Waste Land* suggests, a priori, that a pagan, who is able to "see" what ordinary mortals seek, and who has "foresuffered all," is a singularly inappropriate Holy Grail quester, who despairs of success, and who suffers as he does at the end of "The Fire Sermon" and in "What the Thunder Said." Yet the clearly labelled voice of Tiresias has a distinct, and in the fullest root sense an intimate, relationship with that speaker, as do the voices like it. Part at least of the apparently incoherent series of snatches of discourse in *The Waste Land* is the working of a brilliantly functional narrative strategy. With that encouragement, one can turn to the remaining bulk of those snatches and consider whether the ultimate speaker of which the various prophetic voices are a coherent part is himself coherent. Reflection on the view that the ultimate speaker is a composite suggests, a priori, that it derives from the apparent absence of such a single coherent entity in a poem in which so many *I*s and *we*s speak so abruptly and discontinuously. It is an admissible explanation, but hardly a justification, of what would have been a feeble procedure in a poem— a procedure that would have resulted from the very opposite of a controlling strategy. But Eliot's complex modernist strategy of point of view in *The Waste Land* is, as I have said, essentially coherent throughout its discontinuous texture and despite minor inconsistencies.

His 1953 lecture, "The Three Voices of Poetry,'" whose published version directly precedes in *On Poetry and Poets* that of the lecture which ironically derogates the Notes ("The Frontiers of Criticism"), never mentions *The Waste Land*. But in the same canny manner, he seems to provide in "The Three Voices of Poetry" a description of the kinds of relationship precisely of *voices* that he created in his poem of three decades before.

He begins abruptly by defining his terms: "The first voice is the voice of the poet talking to himself—or to nobody. The second . . . of the poet addressing an audience . . . . The third . . . when he is saying . . . what he can say within the limits of one imaginary character addressing another imaginary character" (p. 96). He confesses that until three years before he had distinguished clearly only two kinds of discourse created by a poet: those of his first "voice" ("speaking for oneself"), and ("in 1938," p. 99) his third ("speaking for an imaginary character," p. 100). The second voice, of "the poet in non-dramatic poetry which has a dramatic element in it" (p. 102), is illustrated neatly: "In *The Tempest*, it is Caliban who speaks; in 'Caliban upon Setebos,' it is . . . Browning talking aloud through Caliban" (p. 102). This newly-identified voice is distinct both from true drama, in which the poet must "find words for several characters differing widely from each other," and "each . . . must be given lines appropriate to himself" (p. 100), and from the poet's "talking to himself—or to nobody," which is "directly expressing the poet's own thoughts and sentiments" (p. 106).

The last clause quoted is quoted by Eliot himself from the definition of "lyric" in "the Oxford Dictionary," and that fact is especially appropriate to what he is about in "The Three Voices of Poetry." He is redefining the three fundamental genres of poetry—the lyric, the narrative (he uses "epic") and the dramatic—rhetorically, as kinds of discourse created by a poet moved by different purposes. While even by traditional definition his third voice is that of drama, his definition of lyric includes all poetry that is primarily declaration or utterance, "*directly* expressing the poet's own thoughts and sentiments" (italics mine), of whatever length, and whether emotional, meditative or philosophical. What remains is the third fundamental genre, that which is primarily narration or report, in which the poet employs neither his first voice nor his third, but that elusive second.

The phrase "directly expressing" encapsulates his rhetorical approach, also represented in his comfortable alternation of the prepositions *to* and *for*. However, the poet, who talks *to* either himself ("or nobody"), a reader of "Caliban upon Setebos," or the audience of *The Tempest*, and who talks *for* either himself or Shakespeare's character, talks "through" Browning's *speaker*. The disparity is heuristic. Immediately after concluding his distinction of the two Calibans, Eliot declares: "It was Browning's greatest disciple, Mr. Ezra Pound, who adopted the term 'persona' to indicate the . . . characters through whom he spoke: and the term is just" (pp. 103–104).

Eliot's new discovery, a second "voice," was the distinction between the poet's providing the truly spoken words of a "personage on the stage" (p. 100) before an audience, and his "speaking through a mask" (p. 104), providing written words to be read, for a surrogate who is not an acted personage, but is himself only words which will be read. It is precisely the distinction between characters in drama and personae in literature—speakers, whether or not identified as named characters, who are not distinctly identified as the poet himself (as they are in the voice speaking in lyric poetry). The second voice of poetry, the voice of epic, is of poetry with a fictional or narrative point of view.

Eliot makes the point that in all true poetry the poet has more than one purpose, with the result that "there is more than one voice to be heard" (p. 109) in the poetry of each genre. And he provides one instance of the third voice—"a dramatic element," in a phrase already quoted—that occurs in poetry of the second:

> In Homer, for instance, there is heard also, from time to time, the dramatic voice . . . . The *Divine Comedy* is not in the exact sense an epic, but here also we hear men and women speaking to us. (p. 105)

And in the passage immediately preceding this one, he declares:

> The second voice is . . . the voice most often and most clearly heard in poetry . . . intended to amuse or to instruct, poetry that tells a story, poetry that preaches or points a moral, or satire which is a form of preaching. For what is the point of a story without an audience, or a sermon without a congregation? (pp. 104-5)

In the light of what has been shown about a new kind of dramatic voice in *The Waste Land*—the voice, identified by the "method" with divinely-inspired prophets, which distinctly *preaches* from within the subject (or subjects) of the poem—Eliot's ostensible catalogue of kinds of poetry of the second voice seems to be like the list of epithets with which he was, in three years' time, to describe the Notes while ostensibly describing those to Marianne Moore's poems. Poetry of the second voice, he says, is poetry intended to amuse or instruct, tell a story, preach or point a moral; satire. The ostensible different kinds of poem that "implies the presence of an audience" (ibid.) are not made grammatically distinct except in the case of "or satire," and the satire meant is promptly identified as "a form of preaching" ("The preacher sought to find out acceptable words"); a description of *The Waste Land* would include all the terms in the list ostensibly cataloguing kinds of poem: comic, didactic, narrative, homiletic, religious, satiric.

If Eliot's catalogue of poetry of the second voice also is slyly intended to describe his own poem of three decades before, is he engaging in wishful thinking? Or do his words really have so consistent a voice? In its opening lines, someone says "we stopped in the colonnade,/And went on in sunlight, into the Hofgarten,/And drank coffee, and talked for an hour." "And we shall play a game of chess," a line in the section with that name, contains a second use of *we*. And a third occurs in the opening lines of "What the Thunder Said": "We who were living are now dying." The problem to be confronted is whether one individual—a distinct character, as people normally are, even if they can hear an inner voice—is speaking of a lot he shares with others, or if the *we* indicates that the poet has created a multiple speaker.

In all cases, the speaker explicitly has companions, one in the latter two, one or more in the first. If more than one, then what follows—the line in German spoken by the "echt deutsch" silly Lithuanian woman, the four by the aristocratic Marie, and the two final ones before the paragraph break that introduces the first occasion on which his inner voice addresses the "Son of man"—are samples of the hour's "talk" of the company. If instead he had only one companion on that occasion he is telling about, then those voices were at other tables, and overheard. The situation is unclear (although the fact that one speaker uses German suggests that they were overheard); but the distinction is immaterial. Other distinctions are both clear and material: of the last two lines, both the English syntax and the personality of the speaker of "In the mountains, there you feel free" are different from those of "I read, much of the night, and go south in the winter."

As in *The Divine Comedy*, "here also we hear men and women speaking to us." But their speech is reported by a narrator who is giving the reader "also, from time to time, the dramatic voice." In *The Waste Land*, Eliot is "talking aloud through" his own Caliban in the way of such fiction as the work of Conrad's that supplied his temporary epigraph—by creating a character-narrator who, like Marlow, tells of a crucial spiritual experience.

Eliot's recording of *The Waste Land* (Caedmon) enables the outer ear to come to the assistance of the inner. For example: his pauses between the snatches of conversation in the Hofgarten are slightly longer than line pauses; all his prophets speak in a slightly oracular voice; and when the quatrain of the "Thames-daughter" seduced in a canoe is succeeded by that of her sister, he stresses the first word: "*My* feet are at Moorgate." But as with the conversation in the Hofgarten, this assistance is required, if at all, by the reader, not by the poem. For example, the first "daughter," associated by a note with Dante's La Pia, uses Dante's word to say that she has been *undone*; the second is distinguished not only by geography, but by her contrasting attitude: "What should I resent?" The next stanza, which is not a quatrain, is spoken by a half-sister, identified by her line about "dirty hands," by the echo of "Moorgate" of the second quatrain in "On Margate Sands," and by the vestige of the song of the *Rheintöchter* which follows it, as much as by Eliot's note referring to "(three) Thames-daughters."

But the individual to whom she speaks had to move east from the Thames to Margate to hear her. The next line, "To Carthage then I came," which a note quotes in its context in Saint Augustine's *Confessions* ("to Carthage then I came, where a cauldron of unholy loves sang all about mine ears"), refers to the unholy loves singing about the ears of the auditor, who reports the songs in "the dramatic voice" of each "daughter" in turn; but it also invokes both the confession of a sinner who redeemed himself, and a place further east. After only the repeated "burning," and Saint Augustine's "O Lord Thou pluckest me out," "Death by Water" begins, with the drowned Levantine sailor held up to the speaker-quester-protagonist as an object lesson by his inner voice, while he continues to move east in his metaphorical journey, toward the sacred river.

In *The Waste Land*, there are three classes of speaker: the enlightened silent voice of an inner consciousness; quoted *dramatis personae*; and an ultimate speaker-protagonist, who experiences the first within himself and the second in the world, and presents both dramatically. One place where all three are juxtaposed in that order is at the end of "A Game of Chess":

HURRY UP PLEASE ITS TIME
HURRY UP PLEASE ITS TIME
Goonight Bill. Goonight Lou. Goonight May. Goonight.
Ta ta. Goonight. Goonight.
Good night, ladies, good night, sweet ladies, good night,
    good night.

The capital letters and portentous words of the bartender's warning, which has interrupted the Cockney woman's sordid account, identify its significance for the protagonist, whose conscience hears in it "words . . . from one shepherd" addressed to him. In the next two lines, the woman and her friends take leave of each other. The final line is an exact quotation from Ophelia in *Hamlet* IV, v, so is simultaneously too learned for the company and a recognizable attribute of the character of the erudite protagonist; furthermore, its speaker is distinguished from them because it is a general comment (much like that of the portentous repeated line) on the account by the woman that the protagonist has just overheard, couched in an ironic reiteration of the leavetaking by the members of the group which allusively invokes a doomed woman; and on the simplest level, it distinguishes the protagonist from them by the difference between their slurred "goonight" and his precise "good night" (a distinction not neglected by Eliot in his reading). The three classes of speaker are quite distinct, and two are rendered dramatically in his narrative by the third.

The protagonist-narrator who recounts dramatically the voices he hears in the world and within himself, also: reflects ("April is the cruellest month"); quotes himself ("I . . . stopped him, crying: 'Stetson!'"); reports his responses to characters whom he has quoted ("–Yet when we came back, late, from the Hyacinth garden,/ . . . I could not/ Speak . . ."); narrates–with exposition, in the manner of narrators ("Madame Sosostris, famous clairvoyante,/Had a bad cold"); quotes from poems and popular songs; reports snatches of poems and songs he has been moved to repeat to himself; meditates; and so on. He tells of having his fortune told by Madame Sosostris, and reports only her words. He is the companion of the neurasthenic woman, and his responses to her are mostly the sort one does not speak aloud.

They also are almost as desperate as her importunings. Like Stephen and Bloom at similar points in *Ulysses*, he is reaching a crisis of despair. Then, having been told "ITS TIME" and said "good night" to the ladies at the end of "A Game of Chess," he ceases his "walking round in a ring," as has been said. He begins, with "The Fire Sermon," the process that will separate him from those lost souls around him in the benighted city, just as Stephen and Bloom, after a time, begin to act. Thus, it is in the opening lines of "The Fire Sermon" that the erudite, reflective, suffering young male protagonist simultaneously: makes explicit the implication of his identity as the "first person narrator" of *The Waste Land*—that he is a poet as well (the poem which is his narrative is his own poem); and indicates that in a poet's way he is about to move from memory to desire, will—as has been said—give expression to the despair he is feeling. In its opening lines he alludes to two prototypes for "The Fire Sermon," one painfully different and the other painfully similar. The former is Spenser's "Prothalamion," which celebrates a progress on the "sweet Thames" of noble sisters and daughters before the (in the words of Spenser's dedication) "double mariage of the two honorable and vertuous ladies"; the other is the psalmist's lament over his exile in Babylon.

All the speaker's subsequent experiences, memories and thoughts: of the creeping rat, Mr. Eugenides, the river sweating oil and tar, Elizabeth and Essex in the time of Spenser, the drowned Phlebas with whom the prophet confronts him in his metaphorical-spiritual pilgrimage, and the tortuous way to "the empty chapel" (where he heard—and reports in that tense, looking back on his waste land—what the thunder said), like all the voices without and within him, take their natural place in "his" apparently autonomous or dramatic poem, the coherent achievement created by Eliot's complex modernist strategy of point of view in *The Waste Land*. That Eliot cut such a brilliant multifaceted gem out of the crude material preserved in the drafts makes his achievement even more impressive.

Eliot's achieved poem of the second voice tells a story and occasionally amuses. But above all it seems to instruct and preach, in the speeches of its inner prophet, the experiences of its character-narrator, even its satire. Yeats said that the poet makes true poetry only out of his quarrel with himself—that of his quarrel with others he makes no more than rhetoric. Eliot not only also employs the poet's third voice in his poem, but, especially in the narrator's reflections and meditations and in the prophets' speeches, "talks" to and for "himself." If he were not personally involved in the spiritual plight of his poet-protagonist, his account of a quest for salvation would be the preaching of the self-righteous, which is to say, the spiritually smug. The stench of sanctimony usually reaches the nostrils very soon, and there is no more trace of it in *The Waste Land* than in *Ulysses*. The last in similarities between them is last because it is different from all the others—a matter neither of theme nor of way of working—and because the discussion of point of view in those two particular works leads inevitably to it. The last similarity concerns the nature of the artist's *invisibility;* this term signifies not absence but unseen presence. Despite what Stephen says in the *Portrait,* the successful artist is not always the remote God of his completed "handiwork," because he is not always "refined out of existence."

Once again, reference to the *Portrait* and "Prufrock" is enlightening. Stephen makes that observation in his aesthetic discourse during the last chapter. It concludes his description (for which he employs the terms Eliot uses more appropriately to distinguish the voices of poetry) of "three forms progressing" in the composition of a work of art out of its creator's experience, that process by which the fully realized or truly autonomous work, he says, is ultimately achieved. The passage is an expression of the familiar modernist concern that motivates the manipulation of point of view, and has its counterpart in Eliot in "Tradition and the Individual Talent." But the discovery about fifteen years ago of a self-glorifying Paterian autobiographical essay, "A Portrait of the Artist," written before the novel *Stephen Hero*, which portrays reality but in which the author is identified fully with the "hero," reveals that Joyce himself underwent the process from "lyric" through "epic" (the mediate state) to the eventual "dramatic" *Portrait*, and is subtly confessing that fact through Stephen's mouth in the very work which is its end product.[92] A similar confession by Eliot can be found in a letter that the youthful creator of a dramatic monologue about an aging man with a ridiculous name who was mortally stricken with indecision and emotional repression wrote to Richard Aldington a few years later; he declares that his own acute emotional trouble is: "due not to overwork but to an aboulie [i.e., abulia] and emotional derangement which has been a lifelong affliction."[93]

In *Ulysses*, the action of the novel itself requires that it take place on June 16, 1904; and yet Joyce subtly made it autobiographical. He first spent an evening with his wife during the time Stephen was with Bloom; the next month he wrote "The Sisters," for the first time making successful art out of his reality, then promptly wrote two more stories for *Dubliners*, and left Ireland. In the novel he presents Bloom as making possible for Stephen during those hours what she had made possible for him.

Eliot's poem about a young poet among the spiritually "dead" in London, written at the time of his emotional trouble, also is more than it is. Although the words are not even the protagonist's own, but those of the third woman in the last part of "The Fire Sermon," what he heard or overheard her say, after she named the place of her seduction, seems more appropriate to the author of *The Waste Land* than to a character likened to the two daughters of the Thames: "On Margate Sands./ I can connect/ Nothing with nothing." And Eliot's alteration of the line from Psalm 137 to "By the waters of Leman I sat down and wept" made it not only a lament over spiritual exile, but also a covert depiction of his emotional state while at Lausanne. After mentioning in *Eliot* the "many voices which say 'I' in *The Waste Land*," Stephen Spender observes: "There is one other voice—the voice of the poet in the poem, who suffers" (pp. 95-96); and a dozen pages later, he asserts about "the man" in the first part of "A Game of Chess" that his series of responses to the woman "projects a character which can only be Eliot himself" (p. 108).

In a different key, two letters to Ford Madox Ford declare "There are, *I* think[,] about 30 *good* lines in *The Waste Land*" and "They are the 29 lines of the water-dripping song in the last part."[94] "Justly celebrated" the song of the hermit-thrush may be, as Eliot's note declares; but it is celebrated by him.

More than the finished poem, the manuscript is personal in specific substance, with its material derived from American settings, its references to "Tom's place," "brother," and "my friend," and a line incorporated from "The Death of the Duchess," which Eliot removed at his wife's request ("The ivory men make company between us"; it followed "And we shall play a game of chess," and he included it in a manuscript he wrote out for an auction sale in support of the London Library in 1960).[95] Perhaps partly for that reason reviewers of the facsimile of the drafts and a series of correspondents to the *Times Literary Supplement* extending through the first months of the jubilee year were moved to discuss autobiographical elements in *The Waste Land* at length, some suggesting the conventional lurid possibilities.[96] In addition, a statement Eliot made a decade after he wrote the poem is placed before the facsimile pages of the volume:

> Various critics have done me the honour to interpret the poem in terms of criticism of the contemporary world, have considered it, indeed, as an important bit of social criticism. To me it was only the relief of a personal and wholly insignificant grouse against life; it is just a piece of rhythmical grumbling.[97]

The Waste Land is a great deal more than that, of course. One reviewer of the facsimile volume, after objecting to Eliot's statement, declares that the poem does not have to be "grumbling" or confession in order to have an autobiographical element, that the external subject with which it deals is "a screen on which is projected the meshed design of the poet's sensibility."[98] And two decades after his announcement that a poem considered "criticism of the contemporary world" "is just . . . rhythmical grumbling," Eliot said in "Virgil and the Christian World":

A poet may believe that he is expressing only his private experience; *his lines may be for him only a means of talking about himself without giving himself away* [italics mine] ; yet for his readers what he has written may come to be the expression both of their own secret feelings and of the exultation or despair of a generation.[99]

It is in this context that we must understand, and emphasize the first two words of, "To me it was only the relief of a personal . . . grouse . . . it is . . . grumbling." Yet Eliot's later statement merely relates the personal and the public in a poet's work more satisfactorily than does the one placed at the head of the facsimile volume; it does not deny what the work is "for him" ("to me"). And in "The Three Voices of Poetry" he articulates his conception of precisely that relationship. As Joyce cannot be dissociated from Stephen Dedalus in *Ulysses*, so the creator of *The Waste Land* is in some essential sense "himself" the poet and spiritual pilgrim in his poem. Specific evidence offered above, his inner personal situation at the time, and his subsequent spiritual history all confirm this deduction.

Both *Ulysses* and *The Waste Land* have full integrity as works of art without the imposition in either of finality on its story. And as the facile open form in some of our current literature compares to this modernist achievement, so precisely does the current autobiographical intimacy compare to the achievement in them of a special invisibility: each writer places his work fully in the world and yet inhabits it. Joyce succeeds in making his invisible presence an elegant triumph of his art; but these two supremely modernist writers have in common the impulse to autobiography normally associated with Romanticism, that great parent which Modernism, the offspring as dialectical antithesis, opposed and eventually supplanted —but inescapably resembled. And this last in a series of similarities between their two works takes its place as the final element of a manifold event of cultural history.

8

MAKING IT NEW

> *Mr. Joyce's book has been out long enough for
> no more general expression of praise, or expostula-
> tion with its detractors, to be necessary; and it has
> not been out long enough for any attempt at a com-
> plete measurement of its place and significance to be
> possible.*

This study is an examination of two particular works of literature, people's
attitudes toward them, and other attendant circumstances and events; it
encompasses an endeavor to contribute to literary history by isolating and
exploring a nexus of specific artistic and behavioral evidence about Modernism, not by essaying a definitive general account of it. Nevertheless,
categorical rejection by certain thoughtful critics of the very concept of a
delineable period properly so named has been substantive and not mere
resistance to innovation. Such rejection must be confronted eventually,
even in a historical effort that intends more affinity with cultural anthro-
pology than with analytics.

The question of the name itself is not trivial, because reality is organized as it is perceived in cultural history no less than in other things: the
shape and even the actual existence of a finite literary period is defined by
the central characterization of it, which is manifest in its name. If indeed
awkward, the coinage "Modernism" out of the root epithet can be considered no more so than "Romanticism" and is distinctly less so than

"Neo-Classicism." More grounds exist for objection to the use of the root itself; and the fact that the familiar phrase "the modern tradition" gives an impression of absurdity reveals those grounds. One manifest cause of the impression is that the epithet denotes an immediate relationship to the present. Yet it is not sufficient cause, nor is the suggested anachronism sufficient grounds for objection: strictly speaking, a fully developed tradition can be of recent origin. Correspondingly, a term signifying recency can be employed for the historical period immediately proximate to ourselves. The seeming absurdity has another cause, however, more subtle and much more important. In addition to the primary sense of "modern," which is wholly relative to the present time of its user and so is ahistorical, the epithet has a sense that is antihistorical: the sense of *modernity*, of newness as a quality attacking the past—attacking precisely tradition.

That sense of the epithet "modern" provides the perspective whereby "modernist" joins "romantic" and "classical" as designations of universal or normative, not historically delimited or descriptive, qualities: the analogy commonly drawn between the literature and culture of the early twentieth century and those of the early seventeenth may be said to be between a romantic and a renaissance modernism. Such a statement may be made and will be understood because to some extent "modernism" names a normative concept, wholly outside historical limits.

However, whereas the other two normative concepts are compatible with periods in literary history (indeed were derived from the appropriate periods), the concept of modernity is, as has been pointed out above, antihistorical—explicitly antagonistic to historical continuity. And that is why calling a finite period "Modernism" has been judged by some not merely a verbally inept temporary expedient but gross error.

One must grant that the epithet "modern" does not lend itself readily to historical use; however, to grant that is not to concede the general case against Modernism as a finite period which in fact is quite properly given that name.

This negative case is put most eloquently perhaps, and its implications are explored most fully, by Paul de Man, in his recent book of "Essays in the Rhetoric of Contemporary Criticism," *Blindness and Insight* (New York: Oxford, 1971). Both the extent of Professor de Man's specific concern with the concept Modernism in his broadly ranging book and his attitude toward that concept are revealed in the fact that his opening and closing pages discredit two popular and contradictory critical "mystifications," as he justly calls them, about the essential quality of Modernism.

One defines that quality as the artists' having turned from their individual consciousnesses toward reality; and the other defines it as the exact reverse. But these deserved rebukes are little more than the setting for his argument: that Modernism is an untenable concept because a paradoxical one. This thesis is presented in the essay before the last, "Literary History and Literary Modernity." Professor de Man articulates the "radical impulse that stands behind all genuine modernity" as distinguished from both "the contemporaneous" and mere "passing fashion" (p. 147), the necessity for that radical impulse in an artist, and the antagonistic but complex relationship between the impulse and the artist's heritage. Then he advances to his argument proper: "the challenge to the methods or the possibility of literary history" (p. 144) inherent in the antihistorical concept of modernity; and he refines his argument by describing the contradiction between modernity and history as, more than that, a significant paradox: "modernity becomes a principle of origination and turns at once into a generative power that is itself historical" (p. 150). In the final essay, "Lyric and Modernity," he relates the fallacy ("mystification") of characterizing Modernism as a turning from reality to this paradox: in art "mimesis and allegory," like "history" and "modernity," are neither sequential nor dialectical but—paradoxically—simultaneous; and "The worst mystification is to believe that one can move"—trace history—from one to the other (pp. 185-86).

These extractions from Professor de Man's subtle and reflective discussion of Modernism do not attempt to represent it, but are limited instead to its exposition of the basic objection thoughtful critics make to the use of the name and to the conception of a finite period. My defense of both can be demonstrated in a slight perversion of his paradox. For, whatever may be the case respecting modernity itself and literary history, it is no paradox to say that *a doctrine of artistic commitment to* that same "modernity becomes a principle of origination and turns at once into a generative power that is itself historical." To place before Professor de Man's paradox those italicized words is to shift the ground of judgment from the intrinsic *logical* and *rhetorical* status of the concept Modernism to that which supplants it as the proper locus: precisely its *legitimacy*—which is to say, its accuracy—as historical description. In the appropriate historical circumstances, although the contradiction of calling the period "Modernism" remains, the name is fully appropriate. What has happened is that the question of internal validity has become irrelevant, simply because the contradiction is not in one's rhetoric but in the historical reality. In other words, objections of this kind to the use of "Modernism" are warranted only if the question of that use is wholly encompassed by logical or rhetorical considerations. If instead that name denotes the essential characteristic doctrines, intentions and unconscious assumptions of the artists whose work dominates the period—if what the name denotes is an artistic -ism of modernity—such objections are not warranted.

That is precisely the case. The epithet "modern" provides a name in literary history despite internal contradiction because the concept involved is not one of a principle (*modernity*) paradoxically obliged to contradict itself when placed in history, but instead one of persons, events and circumstances in history affected by and committed to that principle—precisely what is signified by the root and suffix of "Modernism." The commitment and its doctrine are nicely encapsulated in Pound's title, *Make It New*; the "it" for the "Guide to Kulchur" was not only one's work, but also the received tradition of art. Perhaps the special fitness of the name for the historical circumstances it describes is the reason why it persists and gains currency, when it failed to do so during the debates of the Ancients and the Moderns in France and England around the turn of the eighteenth century, or at any other time.

The suffix is, no less than the root, legitimated by the reference of Modernism to a doctrine and program. To speak of a work as modernist is not to define the work reductively but to specify its historical association. It is our awareness of certain doctrines, intentions and unconscious assumptions of their time that tells us the ways in which *Gulliver's Travels* is neoclassical and Byron's *Don Juan* is romantic; and we would be informed about each work by their opposite historical circumstances if their dates of composition were reversed, would be directed to romantic characteristics in *Gulliver's Travels* and Augustan ones in *Don Juan*. We would be more informed about those specific works than about most others of the time of each in such a case, but only relatively more informed. All works of art are only partly characterized as of their respective periods, even when those periods (and the movements which engendered them) are most appropriately named, because the names designate doctrines, intentions and unconscious assumptions, and so at most designate characteristics of works and tendencies in them that are related to those things, rather than the totality of any work of art. As was said in the opening pages of this study, good art never matches its manifestos.

Our conceptualizations of periods are clearly inadequate as definitive encompassing categories for individual works; it is in the context of this inadequacy that all remaining substantive objections to the concept Modernism are seen to be true, but the reason for those objections to be endemic in the whole endeavor of literary history.

That endeavor remains valid and profoundly necessary. When more than the recital of facts, history is generalization. But to generalize is not necessarily to lie; to generalize about the past can be instead to mythologize. In the opening pages the statement also was made that literary periods are precisely myths, persuasive generalizations about literature during some portion of past time which are neither demonstrable fact nor demonstrable fiction. It is with the object of contributing to some such account that one asks the general question which this study raises: What effect did the advent in 1922 of those profoundly linked and quickly apotheosized works of English literature, *Ulysses* and *The Waste Land*, have on the subsequent shape of our culture? The historical force of the event can be only guessed at. But the era was one to inspire historiographical metaphors like "ferment." It was a time conducive to a "watershed." And in English literature, significantly, the very year that began with the publication of *Ulysses* and ended with the publication of *The Waste Land* also produced an unusual number of books by both distinguished traditional writers and their generally younger modernist contemporaries. Presumably, Lewis's *Babbitt,* O'Neill's *Anna Christie* and *The Hairy Ape,* and the works by Masefield (three), A. E., Blunden, Dunsany, Dreiser, Wells, Ellis, Wharton, Millay, Masters, Beerbohm, de la Mare, Maugham (two), Cather, Glasgow and Upton Sinclair would not have moved the balance a great deal either way by themselves; but such a partial list indicates the vigor of literary activity. Nineteen twenty-two was also the year of Harris's *My Life and Loves,* Galsworthy's *Forsyte Saga,* and Housman's *Last Poems* on the one hand, and of Mansfield's *Garden Party and Other Stories,* Cummings's *Enormous Room* and Sitwell's *Facade* on the other. Belloc, Chesterton, Priestley, Bennett, and George Moore all published books; and so did Forster, Woolf, Middleton Murry, Huxley, Sandburg, Graves, Aiken, Amy Lowell, Stein, Conrad, and Hardy (*Late Lyrics and Earlier*). There were two books by Fitzgerald, three by Lawrence, four by Yeats.[100] Indeed "1922 seems the great year of our time," as R. P. Blackmur declared in "Lord Tennyson's Scissors."

Literary productivity was abundant in the immediately surrounding years as well. And into this situation at its height—in 1922 itself—with the new already contending vigorously against the old, *Ulysses* and *The Waste Land* were introduced, to be enshrined immediately as the supreme exempla of the modernist novel and poem in the language, through the attacks of the detractors of Modernism no less than by its devotees. This was so even though they did not serve in any important way as specific models—not even for the subsequent work of their own creators. And they did not serve in that capacity despite the fact that other modernist writers seem to have been less mystified by them than readers and critics.

That is a strange set of facts, and I have endeavored to isolate some of the reasons for them. One reason is the relationship to the two works, especially to *The Waste Land*, of a man who seems a central figure in a more or less self-conscious movement, Ezra Pound. Another is the influence of Joyce's novel on Eliot, attested as much by the threat Eliot saw to his integrity as an artist as by actual marks of *Ulysses* on *The Waste Land*. But the major reason for their common role in the culture of a half-century ago must be the great number and range of similarities between them whose nature indicates confluence rather than influence, similarities that are made more significant by the fundamental differences between a baroque and sensual work of art and a mostly parsimonious and ascetic one.

There are the similar embodied thematic assertions about civilization, a meaningful life for man, and the cosmos. There are the even greater similarities of artistic practice: the extensive use of the "method" of allusion; the common body of things alluded to; the element of working play (influence is most possible in this case); the pattern of action whereby the (similar) predicaments of the protagonists are presented in a diurnal situation which is then succeeded by a quest; the ending without finality; the disruption of linear progression; the concealment of authorial voice; the subjects' consciousness as the field of action in both. And there is the fact that in each work its creator is invisible but present. These constitute a list of singular—almost remarkable—extent and scope. It is a catalogue of concerns and ways of working which, although it does not comprise all the elements of modernist literature by any means, comprises enough of them, and sufficiently characteristic ones, for the appearance of two such commanding works in 1922 as *Ulysses* and *The Waste Land,* with this catalogue in addition to the external things mentioned in common between them, to be a crux of cultural history.

In other words, although myths are not susceptible of proof, the reception and subsequent status of *Ulysses* and *The Waste Land*, the sponsorship of them, the influence of one on the other, above all the range of similarities and the nature of the similarities between the two works of which these other things were true, seem in some measure to confirm the myth of a distinct phase of our civilization that is being called Modernism, and to demonstrate the sort of thing Modernism was.

NOTES

1. In the Introduction to *T. S. Eliot: The Waste Land, A Casebook,* ed. C. B. Cox and Arnold P. Hinchliffe (Nashville: Aurora, 1970), the editors write of "the transformation of the poem into a myth" (p. 14). In *"Ulysses* and the Age of Modernism," in *Fifty Years: Ulysses,* ed. Thomas F. Staley (Bloomington: Indiana Univ. Press, 1974), pp. 172-88, Maurice Beebe declares: "Joyce's book has taken on the stature of *the* modern myth" (p. 184). He also describes *Ulysses* as "perhaps the single most inclusive and important text of literary Modernism as an independent and autonomous movement" (p. 186).

2. Frank Kermode, "The Modern Apocalypse," pp. 93-124, in *The Sense of an Ending* (New York: Oxford, 1967); the quotation is on p. 103. See also "Modernisms" (chapter 1: "The Modern"), in his *Continuities* (London: Routledge and Kegan Paul, 1968).

3. Monroe K. Spears examines this matter in his recent book, *Dionysus and the City: Modernism in Twentieth-Century Poetry* (New York: Oxford, 1970).

4. " . . . whereas such a poem as *The Waste Land* draws upon a tradition which imposes the necessity of form, though it may have none that can be apprehended without a disciplined act of faith, a new modernism prefers and professes to do without the tradition and the illusion" (*Continuities,* p. 12).

5. The letter is dated 8 and 9 July 1922 (*The Letters of Ezra Pound: 1907-1941,* ed. D. D. Paige [New York: Harcourt Brace, 1950], pp. 178-82, p. 180).

6. I am indebted to Hugh Kenner for this information.

7. Letter of 30 September 1914, *Letters of Ezra Pound,* p. 40. For Pound's meeting with Eliot, see Charles Norman, *Ezra Pound* (New York: Macmillan, 1960), pp. 163, 165-68.

8. Letter of 23 March 1914, *Letters of Ezra Pound,* p. 34.

9. Letter of 18 February 1915, *ibid.,* p. 51. His letter to Joyce, dated 15 December 1913, is in *The Letters of James Joyce,* vol. 2, ed. Richard Ellmann (New York: Viking, 1966), pp. 326-27.

10. See Introduction, *T. S. Eliot, The Waste Land: A Facsimile and Transcript of the Original Drafts Including the Annotations of Ezra Pound,* ed. Valerie Eliot (New York: Harcourt Brace Jovanovich, 1971), p. xii. Subsequent references to this book will be to *"Facsimile."*

11. An accidental enrichment that results occurs in the seduction scene in III: when the rhyming lines of the first two of the final quatrain were dropped, the result was a

Shakespearean sonnet, of which the climax of the sedution is the octave and Tiresias' comment is the sestet, with the final "couplet" appropriately discordant (11. 235-48).

12. "The following year [1922], *Ulysses* at last read as a whole, Pound finally determined what he was doing in the Cantos" (Hugh Kenner, *The Pound Era* [Berkeley: Univ. of California Press, 1971], p. 381). See also Forrest Read ed., *Pound/Joyce: The Letters of Ezra Pound to James Joyce, with Pound's Essays on Joyce* (New York: New Directions, 1967), pp. 193-94.

13. This is done in *A Recent Killing*, by Imamu A. Baraka (LeRoi Jones). It appears from internal evidence to be an earlier work.

14. Herbert Howarth, *Notes on Some Figures Behind T. S. Eliot* (Boston: Houghton Mifflin, 1964), p. 245.

15. Richard Ellmann, *James Joyce* (New York: Oxford, 1959), p. 509. For Joyce's comments about Eliot see also pp. 502, 509-10.

16. See F. O. Matthiessen, *The Achievement of T. S. Eliot*, 3rd ed. (New York: Oxford, 1959), p. 135, and Marvin Magalaner and Richard M. Kain, *Joyce: The Man, the Work, the Reputation* (New York: Collier, 1962), pp. 275-76. Eliot's letter to the *Times* and the one he "might have written" were published under that title in *Horizon* 3 (March, 1941) and reprinted in *James Joyce: Two Decades of Criticism*, ed. Seon Givens (New York: Vanguard, 1948), pp. 468-71; the quoted passage appears on p. 468.

17. See *James Joyce*, p. 542. A detailed account of Eliot's involvement with *Ulysses* is given in Robert Adams Day, "Joyce's Waste Land and Eliot's Unknown God," in *Literary Monographs*, vol. 4, ed. Eric Rothstein (Madison: Univ. of Wisconsin Press, 1971), pp. 137-210, on pp. 179-88; I am indebted to A. Walton Litz for drawing my attention to this monograph.

18. Virginia Woolf, *A Writer's Diary*, ed. Leonard Woolf (New York: Harcourt Brace, 1954), 349. The recollection in 1941 was of a conversation that presumably occurred before 7 September 1922, since her entry under that date mentions "Tom's praises" (p. 49). See pp. 48-49 for her own first and subsequent reactions to *Ulysses*, and for negative and additional positive comments by Eliot.

19. *James Joyce*, p. 542. The specific context of the comment is the nighttown chapter, and it may actually apply only to that; the letter is printed in Day, p. 183.

20. The letter is dated 9 May 1921. The reference to Lausanne is from a letter to Quinn dated 25 June 1922. See Introduction, *Facsimile*, pp. xx-xxi, p. xxii. These and many other passages dealing with *The Waste Land* in the correspondence of Eliot and Quinn are reproduced in B. L. Reid, *The Man from New York* (New York: Oxford, 1968), pp. 489, 534-40.

21. See William York Tindall, *A Reader's Guide to Finnegans Wake* (New York: Farrar, Straus and Giroux, 1969), pp. 33, 60, 78, 102, 142, 181-82, for citation and discussion of relevant passages of *Finnegans Wake*. Professor Tindall declares that Joyce "always insisted that Eliot stole *The Waste Land* from *Ulysses*" (p. 60). And for a highly ingenious account of references to *The Waste Land* in *Finnegans Wake*, and of Joyce's resentment, see Nathan Halper, "Joyce and Eliot: A Tale of Shem and Shaun," *Nation* 200 (1965), 590-95. See also Day, p. 224 (n. 106).

22. On 15 August 1925. The letter incorporating the poem is printed in *The Letters of James Joyce* [vol. 1], ed. Stuart Gilbert (New York: Viking, 1957), pp. 231-32.

23. T. S. Eliot, *Selected Essays*, new ed. (New York: Harcourt Brace, 1950), p. 182. The essay, "Philip Massinger," was first published in 1920.

24. Letter of 23 December 1931, *Letters of James Joyce* [vol. 1], p. 310.

25. Stuart Gilbert (and Ernst Robert Curtius) noted that both works employ the motif of a drowned man; see Gilbert, *James Joyce's Ulysses*, 2nd ed. (New York: Knopf, 1952), pp. 122-24.

26. Professor Day's recent monograph is the most extensive and sophisticated study, and his principal antecedent was Giorgio Melchiori (see n. 28). Other essays more or less devoted to the subject are: Halper (see n. 21); Thomas M. Lorch, "The Relationship between *Ulysses* and *The Waste Land*," in *Texas Studies in Literature and Lang-*

uage 6 (1964), 123-33; and an account of similarities without attribution of influence, Claude Edmonde Magny, "A Double Note on T. S. Eliot and James Joyce," in *T. S. Eliot: A Symposium* . . ., ed. Richard March and Tambimuttu (1949; rpt. Freeport, N. Y.: Books for Libraries, 1968), pp. 208-17. A more complete bibliography would include also: "*The Waste Land* and Joyce," Howarth, pp. 242-46, especially pp. 243-45; Matthiessen, pp. 39-40, 44-45; George W. Nitchie, "A Note on Eliot's Borrowings," *Massachusetts Review* 6 (1965), 403-6; Grover Smith, Jr., *T. S. Eliot's Poetry and Plays* (Chicago: Univ. of Chicago Press, 1956), pp. 60, 79, 84-85, 313 (n. 17); and Spears, pp. 78-79. I am indebted to most of these and to Professor Melchiori's essay for some ideas.

27. Stanley Sultan, *The Argument of Ulysses* (Columbus: Ohio State Univ. Press, 1964 [5]), pp. 51-62.

28. Giorgio Melchiori, "*The Waste Land* and *Ulysses*, " *English Studies* 35 (April, 1954), 56-68; summarized in Magalaner and Kain (see n. 16), p. 221.

29. Melchiori, pp. 57, 61.

30. *Ibid.*, p. 66. In discussing the criticism of Eliot's borrowings in *Finnegans Wake*, Mister Halper repeats this attribution of Eliot's reference to decayed teeth (p. 593, col. 1), and Professor Day infers from him that Joyce "seems to have believed" it as well (p. 188). Joyce "was a man not without malice" and "envy," as Mister Halper says (p. 594, cols. 2 and 3); but he was not silly.

31. Howarth, p. 243.

32. "Eliot said this passage was 'pure Ellen Kellond' " (*Facsimile*, p. 127).

33. *Facsimile*, p. 12 (13). The first instance is on p. 8 (9).

34. *Selected Essays*, p. 183. Professors Lorch and Nitchie assert that in general Eliot's borrowings were unconscious (see Lorch, p. 132, and Nitchie, p. 405).

35. The dirge is at V, iv, 92-101, 104-5.

36. V, iv, 88-90.

37. *The Waste Land*, ll. 218-220; *Ulysses*, Random House ed., p. 49; reset ed. (1961), p. 48.

38. *Facsimile*, pp. 113 and 115 (112 and 114), p. 130.

39. See Professor Ellmann's table, *James Joyce* p. 456.

40. *The Argument of Ulysses*, pp. 277-301. Professor Day's monograph ingeniously links together: thunder; rain; the drowned man and dog; the digging dogs; and the "man in the macintosh" of *Ulysses* and Eliot's "hooded figure."

41. John Hayward dates it "slightly later" than the spring of 1910 in his Introduction to *Poems Written in Early Youth by T. S. Eliot* (New York: Farrar, Straus and Giroux, 1967), p. ix. Stephen Spender suggests 1911 in *Eliot* (Glasgow: Fontana/ Collins, 1975), p. 91.

42. In a paper, "The Urban Apocalypse: *The Waste Land* Fifty Years After," presented at the English Institute 4 September 1972 and published under its short title in *Eliot in His Time*, ed. A. Walton Litz (Princeton: Princeton Univ. Press, 1973), pp. 23-49. (In another essay in the volume, Dame Helen Gardner sets out her different "theory of the composition of *The Waste Land*.") I am indebted to Professor Kenner for providing me with a text, and to the paper itself. It is worth recalling that he suggested long ago that the final form of *The Waste Land* was not in fact "foreseen by the author." See *The Invisible Poet: T. S. Eliot* (New York: Mc Dowell, Obolensky, 1959), pp. 148-50.

43. The *Ezekiel* reference is in "Son of man"; see *Isaiah*, 32:2, 13, 15, 18-20.

44. The label has been preserved with the drafts in the Berg Collection of the New York Public Library and is reproduced in Harvey Simmonds, *John Quinn: An Exhibition to Mark the Gift of the John Quinn Memorial Collection* (New York: New York Public Library, 1968), facing p. 11.

45. *Letters of Ezra Pound*, p. 169. I owe this observation to Professor Kenner's paper; see *Eliot in His Time*, p. 44. Grover Smith also discusses the late development of the title, in "The Making of *The Waste Land*," *Mosaic* 6 (1972-1973), 127-41, 130-131.

46. The ribbon and carbon copies bear the confusing evidence of having been passed

back and forth between them. For example, changes by Eliot himself to the ribbon copy, such as his revision to "demotic (French)" in line 98, were added by Pound to the carbon copy; yet Pound refers on the ribbon copy to alterations and comments he had made on the carbon copy.

47. Presumably it was a portable typewriter belonging to the Eliots. Some of the early poems included among the drafts were typed on it.

48. Professor Kenner makes this point in "The Urban Apocalypse," in *Eliot in His Time*, pp. 24-25, as does Professor Smith in "The Making of *The Waste Land*," pp. 132-33. It is possible that the first two sections were written before the third and typed up later at Lausanne; but that typing sequence is unlikely, and Eliot's statement would put more than the last two sections at Lausanne. For the relevant dates, see *Facsimile*, pp. xxi-xxii.

49. For some reason, neither of the last two sections is numbered on the typed drafts.

50. See *Facsimile*, p. 24 (25).

51. See *ibid.*, pp. 48, 50, 52 (49, 51, 53). The six lines connecting the passage with the portion of "Death by Water" represented by typed and edited drafts, ll. 259-65, were written early; they have two lines transposed and a phrase excised, otherwise are what Eliot pencilled on the upper half of a sheet of paper which bears no comment by Pound; see *ibid.*, p. 36 (37).

52. See *Letters of Ezra Pound*, p. 169, and *Facsimile*, Introduction, p. xxii. There was at least one subsequent fair copy, probably that used by the printers; see *ibid.*, p. xxiii. The drafts cannot be arranged to result in a nineteen-page text, and do not fully correspond to the final poem anyway.

53. Helen Gardner, *The Art of T. S. Eliot* (New York: Dutton, 1959), pp. 84-85; the comparison of the two works extends to p. 88.

54. See, e.g., the review of *The Argument of Ulysses* in the *Times Literary Supplement*, May 23, 1968, p. 526, cols. 3-4.

55. Richard Ellmann quotes from and discusses Yeats's remarks in *Eminent Domain* (New York: Oxford, 1967), pp. 50-51.

56. The critic is Simone Téry, and their exchange is quoted in *The James Joyce Yearbook*, ed. Maria Jolas (Paris: Transition Press, 1949), pp. 189-90. For discussions of the use of allusion in *Ulysses*, see: *The Argument of Ulysses*, pp. 118-22; and Weldon Thornton, "The Allusive Method in *Ulysses*," in *Approaches to Ulysses*, ed. Thomas F. Staley and Bernard Benstock (Pittsburgh: Univ. of Pittsburgh Press, 1970), pp. 235-48. Professor Thornton uses Eliot's essay in his discussion.

57. "I still, after forty years, regard his poetry as the most persistent and deepest influence upon my own verse . . . ." "What Dante Means to Me, " *To Criticize the Critic and Other Writings* (New York: Farrar, Straus & Giroux, 1965), p. 125. See also, in his long essay "Dante," the passages on pp. 213 and 228-29 of *Selected Essays*. The most recent treatment of Eliot's relationship to Dante is by a Dante scholar: A. C. Charity, "T. S. Eliot: the Dantean Recognitions," *The Waste Land in Different Voices* (ed. A. D. Moody), (New York: St. Martin's Press, 1974), pp. 117-56. For Joyce's attitude see, e.g., Mary T. Reynolds, "Joyce's Planetary Music: His Debt to Dante," *Sewanee Review* 76 (1968), 450-77, 451-52; and *James Joyce*, p. 2.

58. See *Facsimile*, p. 128, and *The Invisible Poet*, p. 146, also pp. xiv, 172-73.

59. Pound made the statement in a letter to his father (see *James Joyce*, p. 523). That Professor Kermode's *Continuities* begins with a piece entitled "Modernisms" and ends with one entitled "Dante" is not really significant; but it is the sort of coincidence that was dear to Joyce's heart.

60. Reynolds, pp. 465-69.

61. *Ulysses*, pp. 25 and 567-68; reset ed., pp. 24 and 583.

62. Lionel Trilling, "On the Teaching of Modern Literature," in *Beyond Culture* (New York: Viking, 1968), p. 3. The essay was originally published as "On the Modern Element in Modern Literature."

63. Spears, p. 71. Stephen Spender observes: "Many of his writings at the time and for some years afterwards . . . show how convinced he was that civilization would collapse," and testifies that Eliot assured him later that that had been his conviction; see *Eliot*, pp. 116-17.

64. *The Invisible Poet*, p. 157. Professor Day makes the point that both works present quests for "rebirth and redemption." But here, as elsewhere, his study treats as a matter of influence what seems to me a similarity that is ultimately thematic, and therefore expressive of similar attitudes (see Day, pp. 143-78).

65. See Stanley Sultan, "An Old-Irish Model for *Ulysses*," *James Joyce Quarterly* 5 (1968), 103-9.

66. Matthiessen, p. 52.

67. *The Invisible Poet*, p. 151. On the preceding page, Professor Kenner says, "we should do well to discard the notes as much as possible." For a recent extreme statement of this attitude, see Anne C. Bolgan, *What the Thunder Really Said* (Montreal: McGill-Queen's Univ. Press, 1973), pp. 32-34.

68. T. S. Eliot, "The Frontiers of Criticism," in *On Poetry and Poets* (New York: Noonday, 1961), pp. 121-22. Professor Kenner's discussion of the Notes (*The Invisible Poet*, pp. 151-52) provided my reference to a sixty-four-page book (it also dates the phrase "bogus scholarship" ten years early). The attribution to Roger Fry is from *T. S. Eliot's Poetry and Plays*, p. 67.

69. See: *Facsimile*, Introduction, pp. xxii-xxiv; Reid, p. 538; and Daniel H. Woodward, "Notes on the Publishing History and Text of *The Waste Land*," *Papers of the Bibliographical Society of America* 58 (1964), 252-69, 256-60. The excerpt from Seldes's letter to the publisher of the *Dial*, James S. Watson, Jr., is on p. 260, and is quoted from William Wasserstrom, *The Time of the Dial* (Syracuse: Syracuse Univ. Press, 1963), p. 104.

70. Letters of 28 July-1 August and 7 September 1922; quoted in *Facsimile*, Introduction, pp. xxiii, xxiv. Valerie Eliot says on p. xxx, "There are no notes."

71. Letter of 21 September 1922: quoted in *ibid.*, p. xxiv, and Reid, pp. 539-40.

72; "T. S. Eliot and I," interview of Timothy Wilson with Valerie Eliot, *Observer* (London), 20 February 1972, p. 21, col. 2.

73. The letter to Bennett is quoted in *The Invisible Poet*, p. 181. The poem, "Sage Homme," Pound's advice, and subsequent discussion, appear in the exchange of letters about *The Waste Land*; see *Letters of Ezra Pound*, pp. 169-71.

74. *Observer* interview, col. 4. If the late Robert Sencourt's often distasteful and inaccurate biography, *T. S. Eliot: A Memoir*, ed. Donald Adamson (New York: Dodd, Mead, 1971), can be trusted in matters of personal reminiscence, it provides corroborating evidence of Eliot's playfulness and sense of humor. See, e.g., pp. 8, 74-75, 78, 108.

75. Nitchie, p. 405.

76. See the complete chart published in *James Joyce Miscellany: Second Series,* ed. Marvin Magalaner (Carbondale: Southern Illinois Univ. Press, 1959), following p. 48. The copy is that which Joyce sent to his first biographer, Herbert Gorman, and accompanies the essay by H. K. Croessman on pp. 9-14, "Joyce, Gorman, and the Schema of *Ulysses*: An Exchange of Letters—Paul L. Léon, Herbert Gorman, Bennett Cerf."

77. *Ulysses*, p. 416; reset ed., p. 423.

78. See A. Walton Litz, "*The Waste Land* Fifty Years After," in *Eliot in His Time.* pp. 3-22, pp. 13-14.

79. *The Odyssey by Homer*, tr. [S. H.] Butcher and [Andrew] Lang (New York: Macmillan, 1930), p. 57.

80. For a less sketchy discussion, see *The Argument of Ulysses*, pp. 377-79.

81. Quoted in Matthiessen, p. 148.

82. *Beyond Culture*, p. 8.

83. See Don Cameron Allen, *Image and Meaning: Metaphoric Traditions in Renais-*

sance Poetry (Baltimore: Johns Hopkins Press, 1960), pp. 158-65. The quotation from Saint Ambrose is on p. 161. I am indebted to Professor Day's monograph for calling my attention to this work; see Day, p. 165 and n. 47. David Ward also mentions the traditional significance of the cock in *T. S. Eliot Between Two Worlds* (London: Routledge and Kegan Paul, 1973), p. 132.

84. See *The Upanishads*, tr. Swami Prabhavananda and Frederick Manchester (New York: Mentor, 1957), p. 112.

85. See *Facsimile*, p. 68 (69), and p. 128; and *Selected Essays*, p. 211.

86. *The Spanish Tragedy*, IV, i, 174-77.

87. Letter to Bertrand Russell of 15 October 1923; quoted in *Facsimile*, p. 129.

88. See, e.g., Barbara Herrnstein Smith, "Closure and Anti-Closure in Modern Poetry," in *Poetic Closure* (Chicago: Univ. of Chicago Press, 1968), pp. 234-260; M. L. Rosenthal, "Poetry of the Main Chance," *The Times Literary Supplement*, 29 January 1970, p. 113, cols. 4-5; Alan Friedman, Introduction, *The Turn of the Novel* (London: Oxford, 1966), pp. xi-xvii. The phrase "the non-assertive conclusion" is from B. H. Smith, p. 258.

89. B. H. Smith, p. 244.

90. *Letters of Ezra Pound*, p. 171; the passage, attributed only to "Conrad," is the one in which Marlow says of Kurtz:

> Did he live his life again in every detail of desire, temptation, and surrender during that supreme moment of complete knowledge? He cried in a whisper at some image, at some vision—he cried out twice, a cry that was no more than a breath:
>
> "The horror! the horror!"

91. See, e.g., *T. S. Eliot's Poetry and Plays*, p. 72 ff. For the view that the speaker is a composite of individuals of both sexes, see, e. g., George Williamson, *A Reader's Guide to T. S. Eliot* (New York: Noonday, 1953), pp. 123-24.

92. James Joyce, *A Portrait of the Artist as a Young Man* (New York: Viking, 1956), pp. 213-15; see also, *The Argument of Ulysses*, pp. 185-86.

93. Letter of 6 November 1921; quoted in *Facsimile*, Introduction, p. xxii.

94. Letters of 14 August and 4 October 1923; quoted in *Facsimile*, p. 129.

95. See, e.g., *Facsimile*, pp. 4 (5), 12 (13), 62 (63), 64 (65), 76 (77), 78 (79); also, p. 126.

96. See, e.g.: the review by Richard Ellmann in the *New York Review of Books*, 18 November 1971, pp. 10-16; the review in the *Times Literary Supplement*, 10 December 1971, pp. 1551-52; and letters in the same periodical: 17 December 1971, from Peter du Sautoy; 31 December, from the reviewer and John Chiari; 14 January 1972, from I. A. Richards and G. Wilson Knight; 28 January, from G. Wilson Knight; 11 February, from David B. Rebmann and Peter Dunn; 18 February, from Anne Ridler, G. Wilson Knight and H. Z. Maccoby; 25 February, from J. Chiari.

97. *Facsimile*, p. 1. Mrs. Eliot also has declared: "The years of 'The Waste Land' were a terrible nightmare to him . . .: if he had seen these drafts, they might have brought back all the horror"; and, "It's sheer concentrated hell, there's no other word for it, and it was the sheer hell of being with her that forced him to write it" (*Observer* interview, cols. 2 and 3).

98. Review in *T. L. S.*, p. 1551, col. 1.

99. *On Poetry and Poets*, p. 137. Precisely this passage is quoted by A. D. Moody in "To fill all the desert with inviolable voice," in *The Waste Land in Different Voices*, ed. Moody (New York: St. Martin's, 1974), pp. 47-66. It is followed by an ingenious reading of the poem as not only personal but also secular: "the waste land is . . . the landscape of an inward desolation. . . . The struggle is to recover feeling through lyrical expression"; and Eliot's "at last finding his own voice in song is the token of the reintegration of the self that had been alienated" (pp. 48-51).

100. Information from Lola L. Szladits, *1922: A Vintage Year* (New York: New York Public Library, 1972).

INDEX